Dear Mia,
Enjoy the joy of life together. Dreams come true one day at a time. Love,
Carter

Career Focus

One day at a time

by Colleen McEvoy

CAREER FOCUS
ONE DAY AT A TIME

Published by   Colleen A. McEvoy
               P.O. Box 11
               Elmhurst, IL. 60126

ISBN: 0-9633810-0-8

Copyright © 1992, Colleen A. McEvoy

All rights reserved. No part of this publication may be reproduced, stored in a retrieval system, or transmitted in any form or by any means, electronic, mechanical, photocopying, recording or by any information storage and retrieval system, without written permission of the Publisher, except where permitted by law.

Printed in the United States of America.

First Printing, Soft Cover

ACKNOWLEDGEMENTS

I dedicate this book to all the wonderful friends and family that have helped me put it all together:

Arnie and Sydell Miller for the opportunity to be part of their dream.

Dr. Lew Losoncy for encouraging me to write.

Carole Lyden Smith for telling me to write from my heart.

Dennis Millard for showing me how to run my salon.

Lynn ("LB") Badessa for the positive input on how to share my thoughts.

Thanks to my salon team for their encouragement and support.

Deb and Larry Meyer, Velma McClean, Linda Topolovec, Dorothy Ries and Patrice Lewis for their great office skills.

My dear sister Mary for her love, dedication and hard work.

And, of course, my two beautiful children, Kelly and Jamie. With their love, all things are possible.

INTRODUCTION

In sharing my thoughts with all of you, I hope that no matter where you are on your journey in life, you'll see there is always hope even when all seems lost. What we choose to believe, will ultimately rule our world.

I have been in the beauty industry for 27 years. I've been through many ups and downs, personally and professionally.

I no longer live an addictive life because of my excessive personality. I have learned to live with personal focus. My spiritual life has freed me of depression, bad relationships and totally addictive behavior.

Taking quiet time each morning and reading daily affirmation books is part of the program I live every day called, Adult Children of Alcoholics, often referred to as ACOA.

My program (ACOA) has taught me to feed the imagination with different thoughts and create a new way of living. In program, we have a saying, "Take what you like and leave the rest." We all have many layers to uncover to reveal who we really are.

This book is written with love for all of the service professionals who are ready to accept joy and light into their lives.

This is a simple approach to life that works for me and I hope, will work for you.

January 1

"Education is hanging around until you've caught on."   *-Robert Frost*

Being in a service career has made me understand that the more we educate ourselves, the easier our lives become.

There are so many different classes offered, the list is really endless.

Psychology classes help us not only to understand others and what makes them tick, it also helps us to understand ourselves and why we react the way we do.

Business classes are a must. Whether your goals are to be an owner, stylist, manager or in any type of service career, the more you learn, the easier your life becomes.

When I went to beauty school years ago, many of my classmates were young people who did not know what career they wanted. I knew back then that I had a dream, a goal, and a plan that never wavered. We must continually educate ourselves for personal and professional improvement.

"For Today We'll Find A Way" *to hang around the right places. We'll catch on! Dream, goal and plan.*

January 2

"When one lives sensibly, thinks positively, and believes in the best outcome, good health, while not guaranteed, is more likely to be achieved and maintained."   *-Norman Vincent Peale*

Good Health Rules of Ruth and Normal Peale:
- Have interesting work to do. Keep active at something worthwhile.
- Eat simply. Keep your food intake under control.
- Go to bed early and get up early.
- Give top priority to walking every day.
- Love God, don't hate anyone, and don't be afraid.
- Never let a sense of guilt fester in you. Get it cleaned out.
- Develop *spirit and soul health*.
- Cultivate the *peace of God* that passes understanding.
- Expect and image good health.
- Through spiritual cultivation, keep your *plus factor* robust.

"For Today We'll Find A Way" *to achieve what we believe.*

January 3

"Gumption is an old fashioned word meaning common sense and the guts to go out and do something with yourself with enthusiasm and character."   *-Norman Vincent Peale*

My mother always says, "If you have enough gumption you can achieve anything." Well, she should know, she raised seven children on her own without any help. She was a waitress and worked while we were in school.

How come one person has trouble taking care of one child and another can raise seven?

Divorce can be devastating for children. We must support them financially, spiritually and emotionally. Only then will we raise happy healthy adults who have gumption.

"For Today We'll Find a Way" *to have the gumption to go for it! Follow your heart with enthusiasm and let your character show through.*

January 4

"It's not how old you are that matters, it's how you are old." 　　　　　　　　　　-Marie Dressler

We have a salon owner in our town that has been a hairdresser for over 50 years. Her name is Val and she has enthusiasm for our business. I've grown to respect and care for her; for who she is. Sometimes she calls me to share an idea, or we get our salons together for a class. It really tickles me that she thinks that highly of me.

Can you imagine if all the hairdressers joined hands and shared our knowledge? What's stopping us? We all have something *special* to offer each other. Remember, united we stand and divided we fall.

"For Today We'll Find A Way" *to let the love and peace of our business flourish in each other.*

January 5

"Whatever we feed into our minds and then nurture will grow!"   *-Jacqueline Small*

One of my goals for the past two years has been to find a healthy relationship.

After a great deal of thought, I developed my criteria for a good relationship, which is as follows:
- Kind.
- Considerate.
- Understanding.
- Spiritual.
- Motivated.
- Prefer that he didn't drink or smoke.

For two years, I dreamed about my goal of a healthy relationship. Now I have a plan. It's time to put my plan into action.

"For Today We'll Find A Way" *to write down what we want and affirm it each and every day.*

January 6

"Live your life and forget your age."
-Frank Bering

Do you have clients that are so controlled that they think that because they are a certain age they have to act a certain way?

We are as old as we feel. If we keep our enthusiasm up and a positive attitude working, we will always be young at heart.

The love of our business and adapting to all the new trends, affords us the luxury of being as young as we want to be.

I have encountered so many people that have become old before their time because they give in to the negatives of life instead of building on the positives.

"For Today We'll Find A Way" *to do something for fun so our little kid can come out and play.*

January 7

"To every disadvantage there is a corresponding advantage."   *-W. Clement Stone*

My friend, Lynn Leston, has a career with an Airline. She is a very loving, caring and unselfish person.

Lynn says the hours are crazy, but she's made many friends and they have adapted together.

The disadvantages are missing weddings, social events, and holidays with family.

The advantages are free trips for her family, good benefits and an opportunity to see the world.

Being the kind of person Lynn is, I'm sure she makes traveling out of O'Hare a pleasant experience.

For Today We'll Find A Way" *to try and find the corresponding advantage when a disadvantage comes into your day.*

January 8

"Lovers, children, heroes, none of them do we fantasize as extravagantly as we fantasize our parents."   *-Francine DuPlessix Gray*

    What we practice we become. We practiced; we became; we are continuing to become each and every day of our lives.
    Have we practiced distrust and resentment? Yet there is another way to find our own truths. If we practice trust we will learn to trust. If we practice forgiveness, we will be free of resentments. If we surround ourselves with winners, we will be winners. If we choose to understand others, our prejudices will leave us. If we choose unconditional love, we will find our peace.

"For Today We'll Find A Way" *to take responsibility for choosing our own direction.*

January 9

"Power is in the ability to act!"
-Carole Lyden Smith

It's time for me to find a healthy relationship. I made a positive affirmation list and hung it on my bathroom mirror.

First I went out to lunch with a man from the building where I live (I got the hives). I figured, how bad could it get in an hour? This was a great risk for me, but I had the courage to go forward. I saw him a couple of more times. A nice guy, but no magic.

Second, I met a fellow in the gas station, first date not bad. But the second date, a sharp stick in the eye would have felt better.

We can't expect to achieve results from our first efforts. The important factor about creating positive experiences, is to keep trying.

"For Today We'll Find A Way" *to set forth the power and act on what we want.*

January 10

"Until you humble yourself and give yourself and your problems to God, you'll never get the answers you are seeking. But when you do, you will."
                             -Norman Vincent Peale

For 40 years, I thought I could control everything around me...people, places and things. I lived with frustration and anger.

I feel that the weight of the world has been lifted off my shoulders. If you've never had the pleasure of knowing someone in a 12-step program, and watching them change, maybe through this book you'll have a glimpse of the beauty of recovery.

I grant you not everyone needs a 12-step program, but I feel everyone at sometime needs a little support. It's so much easier to get through the tough times with the support of friends.

"For Today We'll Find A Way" *to let go of our egos long enough for some humble answers.*

January 11

"An in-depth positive attitude wins over all difficulties. So keep it going...always keep it going."
　　　　　　　　　-Norman Vincent Peale

　　My specialness is putting others at ease. I have never met someone that I couldn't make feel comfortable and important. This isn't an ego thing it's a positive attitude and a thankfulness that I can help others.

　　In the past, when I dealt with depression, I was consumed with my own problems. I can honestly tell you what brought about the change for me:
- Getting myself focused.
- Letting my spiritual life guide me.
- Learning to love unconditionally.

"For Today We'll Find A Way" *to keep our positive attitude going and going and going...*

January 12

"If you want to cultivate a desired attitude, you may do so by acting as if you had it." -William James

One of my special team members came to me right after I lost a well seasoned designer. Her name is Cari Cunningham.

Cari pitched in and built her clientele from the one our previous designer had left.

Some months later, I heard Cari telling Kelly and Stacy, "Boy I was scared. She was a hard act to follow, but I faked it till I made it."

Her enthusiasm and love for our business has brought Cari far. It goes to show you even if you make a few mistakes, if your heart is in the right place your clients will go along.

Personality is a big reason a client will request a certain designer over another. A lot of people can cut hair.

"For Today We'll Find A Way" *to not fear change...fake it till you make it.*

January 13

"We, alone, control our personal destiny."
-Jacquelyn Small

One of our clients, Brandy Cannella, told me she wanted to fix me up with her boyfriend's dad. I was apprehensive about a blind date but told her to have him call me. Since my first 2 attempts at a healthy relationship were unsuccessful, I made small revisions to my list for a good relationship:
- To be kind.
- To be considerate.
- To be honest.
- To be spiritual.
- To be self-motivated.
- To have a sense of humor.

Bob Walker called me every day for a week and said, "What's the worst that could happen - we'll be friends." He picked me up and over dinner we both discussed our 'lists' for a good relationship. He's so nice I know we'll see more of each other. It was such a comfortable evening.

"For Today We'll Find A Way" *to plan our personal destiny.*

January 14

"I respect faith, but doubt is what gets you an education."   *-Wilson Mizner*

All my life, I was searching for a better way. Self help books helped me to start to peel away the many layers to get down to who I really am.

A certain amount of who we are, I feel, is conditioned by the way we are raised and how much love and affection we are shown. Our role models also have great impact on the path we take.

Through self discovery, we can make conscious positive changes in our lives. We have the power within to change anything we don't like. I feel nurturing our inner child can be very self healing.

"For Today We'll Find A Way" *to soothe our doubts through faith and education.*

January 15

"A new way of life, is going within for inspiration."
-Colleen McEvoy

My blind date, that Brandy arranged, called and we talked. He seemed nice. He called again and I was still intrigued. We made a date for Saturday night.

I was nervous all day wondering about his expectations. I also wondered how he would fair on my list of what it takes to be a good person.

I only had one hive on my neck when he arrived. We went to dinner at his friend's Italian restaurant and we shared life stories. We shared each other's business philosophies. We talked about our children. He told me he loves red hair, and our wants seemed to be similar. I know deep in my heart, I have made a new friend.

"For Today We'll Find A Way" to take a little risk and go with our new way of life.

January 16

"I have never seen a person grow or change in a constructive direction when motivated by guilt, shame, and/or hate." -William Goldberg

Have you ever been on a diet and cheated? It's the old snowball effect. I ate it; I feel guilty; I should be ashamed of myself; I'm so fat; I hate myself.

As we grow through the many rough spots, the best we can do is to love ourselves as we are. Nurturing our inner child is one of the keys to positive change and personal growth.

We are all okay. So, when one of our many clients brings us homemade goodies because she loves us, we indulge and have one...no guilt. Moderation is the surest way to redesigning our bodies.

"For Today We'll Find A Way" *to search for our own peace. Write down all the things we don't like about ourselves, burn it and let it go.*

January 17

"I accept the universe."   *-Margaret Fuller*

    To accept something is to receive it willingly, with a happy heart.

    We all, each and every one of us, are here for a reason. We can each make a difference in this great universe. I've been teased about saving the world, but I know deep down in my soul, I will make a difference in the lives I touch. There is so much goodness to see if we open our eyes wide and try and understand the next person. We haven't walked in their shoes, so how can we judge what has brought them to where they are?

"For Today We'll Find A Way" *to open our hearts willingly and accept the good we can do for each other.*

January 18

"A man (woman) of courage is also full of faith."
-Cicero

Do we have the courage and faith to stand up for our convictions? The more our faith strengthens, the more courage we have for our journey.

Each day we have the courage to live what we believe: to achieve inner peace and complete focus, we look deep down in our heart and soul.

We have to spend less time beating ourselves up and more time looking at our positives. We'll always do better by encouraging ourselves.

When I look back at how I started, a baby step at a time, I am sure anyone can find their focus if they really try.

"For Today We'll Find A Way" to have the courage to find our own faith. Love and peace will be ours.

January 19

"The price of greatness is responsibility".
-Winston Churchill

As soon as we each take responsibility for our own destiny, the easier our lives will become.

We can create our own careers. What we need to achieve success is available. We just need to make the committment.

Ten years ago, life was very different for me. I set my dreams, wrote down my goals and made my plan. Along the way, I joined Adult Children of Alcoholics, a 12-step program.

When we make up our minds, we become focused. With help from above, we can achieve what we believe.

"For Today We'll Find A Way" *to be responsible for our own greatness.*

January 20

"Ethics - a set of rules laid out by professionals to show the way they would like to act if it was profitable."   -Frank Dane

When running a business, a profit is important. What kind of ethics are we teaching about life when we offer to help the less fortunate?

My daughter Kelly gave a young man named Brad a haircut on Saturday. He was one of the homeless people we have given free service in the past. Brad would stop by periodically to say hello and give us an update on his progress. He is now working and paying his own way.

When we provide services for the homeless, our regular clientele are unaware of who the homeless are, because they pay us with a card that entitles them to a free service.

"For Today We'll Find A Way" *to understand how we can help someone's self-esteem. Only when we believe, can we achieve.*

January 21

"All is well that ends well."   *-John Heywood*

Dr. Lew Losoncy has said, "In the game of life, nothing is less important than the score at half-time, and we can't tell the score, if there's no goal posts."

We must have clearly defined goals, written down and affirmed each day, to achieve them.

What do you want your epitaph to read? For me, I don't want to be the best hairdresser (as if there could be only one). I want people to say, "Colleen was the best person she could be!" Ahh, success.

"For Today We'll Find A Way" *to see what our legacy would be if today was our last day?*

January 22

"Character building begins in our infancy and continues until death."   *-Eleanor Roosevelt*

My daughter Kelly has blossomed into a beautiful woman. She has impeccably high standards, and she has self-esteem that will bring her nothing but happiness.

Kelly has been through much emotional growth It was hard for her when her father and I divorced. She believed in me enough to realize we would all be happier. She is such a genuine person. Her love of children is her strength.

It might seem that being her mother, I have shadowed the truth. Ask anyone that has had the pleasure of knowing her. She is a special young woman and the light of my life.

"For Today We'll Find A Way" *to tell our children what is right with them. Happy Birthday Kelly!*

January 23

"To change a human being is the greatest feat imaginable because the most complicated entity in the world is man himself." -Norman Vincent Peale

Once you get the hang of how to encourage people, it's wonderful to take a step back and watch people grow.

The king of encouragement will always be Dr. Lew Losoncy. He is so very special and our industry is so lucky he chose to guide us.

After Dr. Lew's first Salon Psychology Program, I was hooked. He helped me understand where others are coming from and gave me the thirst to learn more.

We are in the business of making people feel good about themselves. It's much easier when you understand different personality types.

"For Today We'll Find A Way" *to help people change, by treating them as if they already have.*

January 24

Take the lead. Be the one to start the relationship."
-Dr. Lew Losoncy

Have you ever felt that there are no strangers, just people you haven't met yet?

I always remind my teammates that the more they talk to all our clients, the more those clients will trust them, as well as their regular stylist. Take the initiative to bond with people wherever you are. That's how I was fortunate enough to build my clientele.

Don't be afraid to compliment someone. Be genuine and you'll touch them in the heart. See what common interests you share. Turn their words into feelings, and people will know you care. The most effective use of body language is a smile. Also, maintain eye contact.

"For Today We'll Find A Way" *to be thankful for the Dr. Lew's who can help us grow with this information.*

January 25

"I discovered I always have choices and sometimes it's only a choice of attitude."   -Judith M. Knowlton

My family seems to be split between being either very optimistic or very pessimistic. I have come to the conclusion that it is a matter of choice.

Here's a short synopsis of a few of my successful cousins.

Dan O'Brien's business is the motivational and inspirational training of salespeople. He couldn't find a company to appreciate what he could do, so he started his own very successful consulting firm.

My cousin Marilyn O'Reilly started as a Kelly Girl assigned to work for the Phil Donahue Show and now runs her own freelance business all over the world in audience coordination.

Joe McMahon has worked for the Chicago Police Department for almost 30 years. He attended law school at night and now is an attorney.

Where there's a will there's an 'A'.

"For Today We'll Find A Way" *to plant a seed deep down in our souls so we can grow to be successful.*

January 26

"The greatest happiness you can have is knowing you do not necessarily require happiness."
                              -William Saroyan

Happiness to me is like a fleeting bird. One has moments of happiness. How would we know life's ups, without the downs?

Living one day at a time has afforded me many of life's pleasures.

In the past, I spent most of my time worrying about the next day, next month, the next year...and missed the moment. The overwhelming fact is that things change daily, and usually the very things that would worry me, would never materialize anyway.

Feeling an internal focus as I begin each day, has brought me happiness I would have never dreamed possible.

"For Today We'll Find A Way" *to become aware of all our options and be able to build a healthy, happy future.*

January 27

"The higher choice will always be a positive one."
-Jacquelyn Small

While preparing for my photo shoot with *Modern Salon*, I got very anxious. Would I do it exactly right? What kind of model? Would she be pleased with the results? A million decisions came to mind. Then as my dear friend Carol Lyden Smith always says, "The first step forward is a step back." I stepped back and asked my higher power for focus and guidance. The shoot was a done deal.

Arlene Tolin picked a beautiful young model named Suzanne, with natural auburn hair, long and straight (very sixties look). I gave her a perm that gave her the look and feel of natural body. I used large rods in the direction of her natural growth pattern. I also used a semi-temporary hair gloss to bring out her natural highlights. She made my layout for February, '91, outstanding.

"For Today We'll Find A Way" to let your higher power guide you to positive choices.

January 28

"We tend to pick select people like ourselves, a very monotonous diet. We tend not to choose the unknown, which might be a shock or a disappointment or simply a little difficult to cope with. And yet, it is the unknown with all of its' disappointments and surprise that is the most enriching."   -Anne Morrow Lindbergh

It's been said, "Birds of a feather flock together." There is comfort in being with people just like ourselves.

On my journey, I've been through so many changes. The one thing that sticks out in my mind is that as I've gotten healthier, so has the company I keep.

Each time we take a risk of the unknown, we have a chance to grow and make our lives more enriched.

"For Today We'll Find A Way" *to be able to see all the possibilities. Take the chance for positive changes.*

January 29

"If you may continually gather yourself together, do it sometime, at least once a day, morning, or evening."   *-Thomas A. Kempis*

It's important to focus ourselves at least once a day. Each morning we can take a few minutes to ask ourselves to make the right choices, and have a successful day.

Being positive, and having inner strength to do what it takes, means to go within for the answers.

It takes a few moments of quiet time away from the radio, TV and the outside world, to find the focus to have a productive day.

When I forget to take my time to focus, my whole day seems off kilter.

"For Today We'll Find A Way" *to start each day with a quiet time to focus, and take on the day with enthusiasm.*

January 30

"I can always be distracted by love, but eventually I get horny for my creativity."   -Gilda Radner

One of the affirmations I said each morning for about two years was, "find a healthy relationship."

As busy as my life always is, I didn't know where I would have time for another realtionship, but after meeting Bob Walker I have made time. He's a kind, caring, and funny guy. Somehow we've incorporated our lives without too much difficulty.

I did have a rough time finding the time to write, but Gilda said it beautifully.

In our industry, there is such wonderful creativity and as we share it with each other, our strength and hope for a better future is bound to be.

"For Today We'll Find A Way" *to share our knowledge is to broaden all of our horizons.*

January 31

"They are able because they think they are able."
-Virgil

My grandson, Zachary, finally got out of the hospital when he was six months old. His name means strength, and with all the odds against him, he made it.

His doctors only gave him a three percent chance of survival. So many people prayed for him, including my clients. When someone has love and support, anything is possible.

Zak pulled out his respirator tube and started breathing on his own. His doctor said, "He must know more than we do."

Miracles do happen each and every day. If we open our eyes, we can see the miracle of life all around us.

"For Today We'll Find A Way" *to be stronger with each and every positive change we experience. Let's **look** for the miracles in life.*

February 1

"Don't bother to just be better than your contemporaries or predecessors. Try to better yourself."   -William Faulkner

A young stylist I know named Kris works for a salon that doesn't let the designers keep client cards, unless they receive a chemical service. Who is that owner hurting?

We must think progressively and keep good records. Direct mail to our own client base is our business of the future.

Clients have a lot of good salons to choose from. What makes our salon special that keeps them coming back?

When I look back to my own salon 25 years ago, I see so many positive improvements and so many more for me to make.

Sharing ideas with other salon owners and designers will help. How many of your stylists have friends that are stylists with whom they could network?

"For Today We'll Find A Way" *to ask each other for new improvement ideas; network to help each other.*

February 2

"We are all alike on the inside."   *-Mark Twain*

What we all want is acceptance. To love one another as we are. Is it too much to ask to accept each other in spite of our shortcomings?

We are each on this earth to accomplish what we will. As our paths cross, is it really up to us to judge one another?

There is a reason we meet each and every person that we encounter. Maybe something they said makes our journey easier. Maybe we give them some kind of comfort.

Let's try and remember that we are all alike on the inside.

"For Today We'll Find A Way" *to take our own inventory and overlook the flaws in others.*

February 3

"Adornment is never anything except a reflection of the heart."   *-Coco Chanel*

In this age of name brands our world is so taken with showing our worth by what we wear. How proud some people are of their labels! The news has shown young people getting killed over sports jackets and name brand tennis shoes.

I've never been a name brand or jewelry person. I wear two rings, one from each of my two children, Kelly and Jamie. They are a reminder of how important my children are to me.

As we dress each morning, let's dress for success. Let's look at the end product without focusing on labels. How we look and dress gives us the feel of success. It also let's others form an opinion of who we are.

"For Today We'll Find A Way" *to dress so it reflects what's in our hearts.*

February 4

"Most people believe they see the world as it is. However, we really see the world as we are."
-Anonymous

Have you ever had the experience of looking back at a bad situation from the past and seeing it much differently than you did originally?

Life is a journey, not a destination. As we learn to grow and learn acceptance of others, we will find our own peace.

We can set our goals to give back to this world what we have been so lucky to have been given. Most of us are lucky to have good health and the ability to make each and every day whatever we choose to make it.

An optimistic attitude is our own free choice. We are lucky to have free will. Look to the world with love - the more we give, the more love we will receive.

"For Today We'll Find A Way" *to look deep in our souls at our world and how we can grow together.*

February 5

"Habit is habit, and not to be flung out the window by any man, but coaxed downstairs a step at a time."
-Mark Twain

When I reflect on where I was ten years ago, I really have so much to be thankful for today.

Through the years, I have read so many self help books. I've been on a self improvement quest since I was in high school. Only in the last five years, after getting involved with Adult Children of Alcoholics, have I started to feel what serenity is all about.

We sometimes have layers and layers to uncover before we can start to get a glimpse of who we really are.

Now I am starting to work on my food addiction. I am most definitely a compulsive overeater. Through the grace of God, I will get help with my powerlessness over food.

If you are lucky enough not to be compulsive, give thanks each and every day. If you are compulsive with anything, find a 12 Step Program.

"For Today We'll Find A Way" *to form good habits together - one step at a time.*

February 6

"The first point of courtesy must always be truth."
-Ralph Waldo Emerson

Sometimes when we're frustrated with a situation, if we go within, we already know the truth of what we must do. When we avoid facing the truth, we end up in turmoil.

There can be great fear in facing the truth in any given situation. Try and always affirm the opposite of fear - courage. When we have the courage to go forward, the truth will appear.

My own point of courtesy is to give each person I encounter a genuine compliment. To make someone feel good about themselves could help them find their own truths.

"For Today We'll Find A Way" *to never be afraid of the truth, for the truth will set us free.*

February 7

"I can live for two months on a good compliment."
-Mark Twain

It is truly amazing how good a compliment feels. If someone tells us we have a beautiful smile, we grin from ear to ear. Each time we smile that compliment might come to mind and it makes us feel good all over again.

Now I ask you, if we can make people feel so good by a sincere compliment, why don't we do it more often?

We can find something to compliment on each and every person we encounter, so why don't we help build self-esteem by telling others what's right with them? Compliment not only our clients, but also our co-workers. It sure makes our day and theirs, more positive.

"For Today We'll Find A Way" to look at everyone and find something to compliment. Everyone will feel better!

February 8

"The Lord gave us two ends - one to sit on and the other to think with. Success depends on which one we use the most."   -Ann Landers

Do we go through each day like robots? Is our client's hair done before they get a chance to ask for a change?

Our success in the salon depends on how we treat our clients, not just on how we do their hair.

If we sit around and complain that there's no business, that will be the fact. If we brainstorm we will come up with many ways to bring people in the doors and hang on to them. Do you send post cards to remind your clients it's time for a haircut? Time for a color or perm? It sure brings clients in more often.

"For Today We'll Find A Way" *to use the right "end" and be successful salon professionals.*

February 9

"The only treasures that are worth saving are those we lay up in the heavens of the mind. The only gold that can be trusted to bring happiness is the gold of the spirit."   -Charles Fillmore

While working the Midwest Beauty Show, I had the pleasure of working with a special lady whom everyone calls 'LB' (Lynn Badessa). She has a real find-a-way attitude.

When we are focused, all that we need will come to us. The last Midwest Show I worked with Carole Leyden Smith, she encouraged me to write from my heart. This Midwest Show, LB helped me with some changes to make my daily book better.

When we are ready, the teacher will appear. When someone cares enough to help us, they give us a piece of themselves.

"For Today We'll Find A Way" *to be all that we can be through the help of friends.*

February 10

"A person's opinion is only as good as his or her information."   *-Colleen McEvoy*

Someone can hurt my feelings only when I value their opinion. The important thing is we can only do our best with the information we've been given.

The most important thing I have learned, on my quest to be the best person I can be, is we are products of the way we were brought up. Our parents were products of our grandparents and so on and so on.

We have all been given a different message as to what love is and how to show it. What message have you given your loved ones? Have we listened to their dreams? Have we encouraged them to reach for the stars? Have we made them realize how special they are to us?

"For Today We'll Find A Way" *to see if our opinions are really our own or were they given to us by someone else? Are these opinions based on truths?*

February 11

"Man will do many things to get himself loved; he will do all things to get himself envied."   -Mark Twain

On my way to my aunt's house, my mom and I were talking and I went the wrong way. We went through five beautiful little towns getting back on route. I enjoy these times with my mom and she loves seeing her sister, so even though we were a little lost, we laughed and enjoyed it.

The homes in these towns were beautiful gigantic mansions. It really makes me wonder, are the people happy inside? Have their values changed? Externally, they live in luxury and nice surroundings.

I do believe no matter where we live we all have crosses to bear. Happiness is such a strange fleeting bird. Finding our own focus will give us the peace within, regardless of our physical surroundings.

"For Today We'll Find A Way" to show love is a beautiful gift, so open our hearts and our minds.

February 12

"The richest love is that which submits to the arbitration of time."   -*Laurence Durrell*

The love of the beauty industry has carried me through some rough times.

Whenever I was having problems in my personal life, I would throw myself into my work. It kept me sane. Somehow when you walk in those salon doors, and keep busy making your clients look and feel good, a sense of peace comes over you.

I often think how horrible it must be to hate your profession. I've had clients tell me they hate going to work each day. I realize how very lucky I am to love my life's work.

"For Today We'll Find A Way" *to recognize how much our industry gives back to us. It's a good feeling to transform destinies.*

February 13

"You cannot help men permanently by doing for them what they could and should do for themselves."
-Abraham Lincoln

Being in a service business, it is really easy to fall in the trap of being a caretaker. We then become the victim.

We all are responsible for our own actions and sometimes when we tend to be caretakers, we do our loved ones a big disservice.

As we move forward in our lives, remember, even in our own families, be it our family of origin or our family in the workplace, the love we give could and should let each of us grow at our own pace. When we want change we must go within and create change in ourselves.

If we want people to act a certain way then we must act as role models and they will be attracted to our way of life.

"For Today We'll Find A Way" *to see that most of life's great lessons are based on attraction, not promotion.*

February 14

"No institution can by itself replace...human love or human initiative, when it is a question of dealing with the suffering of another."   -John Paul II

I found this quote hanging on the wall at a hospital. My reason for being here is my dear boyfriend Bobby was brought in with an aneurysm. He has to have brain surgery.

Bobby is my soul mate. From the moment we met, our lives were different. He is kind, genuine and loving, and makes my heart smile.

It's a horrible experience to see someone you love suffering.

My team took over the salon and pitched in so I could be at his side. They all love Bobby as I do.

"For Today We'll Find A Way" *to ease the suffering of those we love.*

February 15

"We are all failures - at least the best of us are."
-James M. Barrie

What right do we have to judge others? Are we free of failure? It is so easy to judge others and their mistakes, but so hard to discuss our own?

The more focused we become, the easier it is to go within for the answers. If we continue to have the same types of failures, it just means we haven't learned yet from our experience.

If we have one bad relationship after another, we have to stop and figure out why we are drawn to people that are bad for us.

Self-discovery has been a rewarding part of my life and I encourage each and everyone to become stronger through self discovery.

"For Today We'll Find A Way" *to learn from our failures and take the strength from our successes. The law of averages - we can't fail all of the time.*

February 16

"6 tease reintroduces the razor, elevates the impact and creativity of vintage '60's color and perm theory, and adds the naturalness of the '90's."
                                        -Dwight Miller

Our business has gone full circle. In the early sixties we worked exclusively with the razor, very little work with our shears.

We never have to grow old gracefully being in our industry. We can look and feel as young as we want to.

It makes me feel so good to teach my young stylists a technique that got me started in the wonderful world of hairdressing.

How many lives have we all touched with our special talents? Wouldn't our world be grey without the dedication of salon professionals?

"For Today We'll Find A Way" *to share old and new ideas so each of us can hone our craft.*

February 17

"Experience...is simply the name we give our mistakes."   *-Oscar Wilde*

Haven't we all said, "If I had only known then what I know now?" I think it's important not to beat ourselves up. We have done the best we could with the information at hand.

I feel I am destined to experience happiness and joy because I have found peace within myself.

If we learn from our mistakes, our experience was well spent. If life gets a little easier each day, then we are growing.

No matter how many mistakes I've made in my life, goodness came through too.

"For Today We'll Find A Way" *to realize that all our life's experience is an intricate part of who we really are. Today is the first day of the rest of our lives.*

February 18

"The mind unlearns with difficulty what it has long learned."   *-Seneca*

During my early years of owning a salon, I made money in spite of not knowing a thing about business.

Through much education and self discovery on how to run a business, I have been lucky enough to grow. The classes are all available, check with local distributors and also junior colleges.

The extra effort we put into our profession will come back to us one hundred fold.

Each and every person we meet could help us network our careers and personal lives.

One of my clients, Becky Hall, found a reasonable loan for my condo.

My first salon loan was from the bank in our small town. The loan officer said he could see I believed in myself so he'd give me the loan.

"For Today We'll Find A Way" *to forget unproductive ways and opt to be positive.*

February 19

"Ten percent of all people want to succeed. Ninety percent of all people are looking for an excuse to fail."   *-Jon Gonzales*

How many of us maximize our potential? Are we willing to take an extra client or are we booked? Do we schedule our work around our social life or do we schedule our social life around our work? Have you ever placed more importance on a social event than your day in the salon?

Jon Gonzales has a lot of good ideas for being more successful in the salon. He says, "Most people fail because of what they don't do." Only ten percent of all hairdressers make over $25,000 a year. Have you made your decision on how much you want to make? Clients are clients wherever you go, the difference is in us.

"For Today We'll Find A Way" *to look over our client list and see what we can do to make our clients look and feel better. The money will follow when we are servicing our clients.*

February 20

"Just think how happy you would be if you lost everything you have right now, then got it back again." -Frances Rodman

We have a homeless shelter in our town and our staff decided to offer their services to the shelter's residents.

It tells me what these girls are made of. They have the faith and gratitude and are thankful that they are not in a homeless situation. We are never totally sure of what life has in store for us.

Some of the homeless have alcohol and drug problems, but many are just people who have fallen on hard times and lost not only their possessions but their self-esteem.

"For Today We'll Find A Way" *to give back to the community that supports us. Our appearance has so much to do with our self-esteem.*

February 21

"We are healed of suffering only by experiencing it to the full."   -Marcel Pronst

My boyfriend Bobby has had his surgery. It ended up being a 13 1/2 hour operation.

It's really hard to relay these feelings on one page but I'll try. The pain he went through was unbelievable. He has malignant hypertension and apparently was born with the aneurysm. During the operation, after they clipped the aneurysm, a blood vessel burst from his blood pressure going so high. Dr. Dan Heffez, his neurologist, said in his 11 years of operating, he has never seen a case like Bobby's. The night of surgery the doctor said, "I've done everything I could, we'll have to wait and see." They said he wouldn't wake up for 24 to 36 hours. He woke up an hour later on the mend.

A miracle happened through prayer.

"For Today We'll Find A Way" *to have a spiritual experience.*

February 22

"Exaggerated sensitiveness is an expression of the feeling of inferiority."   *-Alfred Adler*

Have you ever known someone overly sensitive? They usually take everything personally and love being the victim.

Isn't it strange, even when you can suggest a way to get better, some people are comfortable with wallowing in self-pity. We are all at different levels of growth. Feeling inferior can surely make someone overly sensitive.

Can encouragement help these kinds of people? I'm sure of it. I think everyone feels inferior at times. If we tell people what's right with them they can build on their strengths.

"For Today We'll Find A Way" *to have an encouraging day. We can give strength to those who need it. Do unto others...*

February 23

"Toleration is the greatest gift of the mind."
-Helen Keller

I have a friend, Lonnie, that I've known since I was 15 while working at a local supermarket to pay my way through beauty school.

She took a risk and let me do her hair my first week on the job in our local salon. Now, I visit her at the local nursing home and try and make her life a little more comfortable. I know in my heart someday, someone will be there for me. When you think life is tough, visit an old people's home and talk with these wise old souls. Their advice? They would have taken more risks.

"For Today We'll Find A Way" *to remember that the opposite of fear is courage.*

February 24

"Optimism is a kind of heart stimulant; the digitalis of failure."   *-Elbert Hubbard*

Success would be easy if we looked at each day optimistically. Say to yourself, "Which of my deserving clients can I step-up to another service."

Each of our clients deserves to look and feel good. Through networking in our salon, we work as a team, suggesting manicures, skin care, color, etc. We not only help sell a service, our clients feel better leaving the salon.

We finally have a really good nail tech named Connie in our salon. She is very good at her craft and I think of her every morning when I wake up and see my beautiful nails. Our clients deserve to smile when they look at their nails too.

"For Today We'll Find A Way" *to optimistically suggest an add-on service.*

February 25

"Link with people. People like people who they think like them." -*Dr. Lew Losoncy*

"We must tap into the power of shared interests and experiences," Dr. Lew suggests. He also said to use we, our and us words to bond with our clients.

It's also important to mirror our clients' actions. If they use facial and hand gestures, so do we. People will identify with us and a bond will be created.

He has also taught us that our professional and financial success, depends upon our ability to motivate others.

Understanding the needs of clients is an important part of client satisfaction.

"For Today We'll Find A Way" *to form a strong link to our clients and they will feel comfortable and then trust will follow.*

February 26

"Enthusiasm is a super important, basic element in successful living. The 'alive' type of personality always goes places when that aliveness is accompanied by positive thinking and solid faith."
-Norman Vincent Peale

Once successful living is a part of your everyday life, there will be no ordinary days.

The beauty of watching the waves on Lake Michigan, off Lakeshore Drive, in Chicago is breathtaking and soothing.

I met a new friend, Jerry Greenburg (of all places) in the Neurological Intensive Care waiting room. His friend had a stroke, my friend had an aneurysm. A common bond, a reason to share some thoughts with each other.

When life deals you lemons, make lemonade.

"For Today We'll Find A Way" *to be an 'alive' type personality.*

February 27

"Twenty-six million Americans are touched by you (hairdressers)."   *-Dr. Lew Losoncy*

We are in a high touch profession. At a Target for Success Program, "How to be a positive influence on others," Dr. Lew reminded us that we are one out of six professions that touch people.

He also feels we are the unsung heros that are with our clients through births, divorce, careers and death. We see them more often than their doctors.

How many clients have you given a first haircuts to and are still doing their hair for their weddings?

Dr. Lew brought to our attention that for some of our clients we are the only one that touches them every week. He said build trust and credibility by being consistent. Do what you say you're going to do at the exact moment you said it would be done. Also, talk about your area of expertise.

"For Today We'll Find A Way" *to picture how many lives you will touch today. Let's be the difference in our clients' lives.*

February 28

"Create a winning feeling in the person. See what's right with people."   -Dr.Lew Losoncy

Dr. Lew is such a wise man and so full of terrific ways to help us. His classes are better than going to a therapist because he focuses on our industry.

He suggests that we focus on a person's assets, as well as to communicate your confidence in the person. If you want someone to develop a trait, treat them as if they already had it.

We must also generate our enthusiasm for their possibilities. If we identify something that is both positive and unique Dr. Lew says it will not only make them feel good, but will make them feel good about themselves.

"For Today We'll Find A Way" *to show our clients how special they are and tell them we care.*

February 29

"Keep going and going, even when nobody seems to notice, because you do."   -Dr. Lew Losoncy

There are so many complex things that make up an individual's personality. We can learn through Dr. Lew's program how to understand where each of our clients and co-workers are coming from.
- Determine a person's sensory style (visual, auditory, or tactile.)
- Determine a person's comfort change level - past (traditional), present (now), future (responsible and in charge of their future).
- Determine a person's motivation source (internal or external).
- Determine the person's comfort level with you.
- Determine whether someone is outgoing or introverted.
With so many things to learn, to be the best salon professional we can be, how can we not educate ourselves?

"For Today We'll Find A Way" *to show we are all so unique Wouldn't it be great to understand how to really get in touch with one another's feelings?*

March 1

"The shoe that fits one person pinches another; there is no recipe for living that suits all cases!"
 -Carl Gustav Jung

Each of us is so very different and special. No one can do exactly what we can, we are unique. What a wonderful world this is that we are not all one of a kind.

Try and remember people's good points and try and over-look the negatives.

We can each choose to bring joy into the lives we touch. Joy to me, means giving of our heart, mind and soul. Can their be more pleasure than to give?

Self centeredness can be so destructful and demeaning.

We can open our eyes and find the beauty in each other and smile from deep down in our hearts.

"For Today We'll Find A Way" to live our own recipe and show our faith and gratitude for what we have.

March 2

"The wise don't expect to find life worth living; they make it that way."   *-Anonymous*

Working at the Midwest Beauty Show is a moving experience. Each and every person I encounter has a special force about them.

I have heard so many positive stories about change in our industry and how it has affected life in the salon.

Giovanni's Full Service Salon is owned by Carol Pupillo in Norridge, IL. Carole and I first met at a convention in Cleveland. She's been in our business for 33 years and her husband has been in the business for 30 years. After our meeting in Cleveland, Carol went home and became ill. She lost both kidneys and dialysis became a big part of her life. She told me her work and the love of her profession and family kept her going.

"For Today We'll Find A Way" to make life worth living.

March 3

"Great is the human heart who has not lost his childlike heart."   *-Mencues*
                                                -4th Century BC

Hair shows are a great source of motivated professionals. I had the pleasure of working with Cindy Bonar (we tease her and call her 'Boner'). She's from Churubusco, Indiana. She told me the reason she likes to work the shows is to give back to the industry that has given her so much.

Cindy has a very progressive salon. She sends out a newsletter to inform clients of what's new in services, products and the neighborhood and about specials being offered. By computerizing her salon, bookwork and mailings are much easier.

As you can see, we don't need to have a big city salon to be innovative and creative. If you go visit Cindy and her team, you'll be openly welcomed.

"For Today We'll Find A Way" *to open our hearts from our child within.*

March 4

"The best way to make your dreams come true is to wake up."   *-Paul Vale'ry*

One of our stylists thanked me the other day for hiring her. Cari said if she wasn't in a progressive salon, she wouldn't be the stylist she is today.

Cari is one of those curious people that wants to know the why's of how things work. Kind of like Elliott Ness, "I want some answers and I want them now."

When we share our knowledge with each other we all grow stronger and benefit.

We are all building dreams and in our business, we can't do it alone.

"For Today We'll Find A Way" *to make our dreams come true. Are we laying the ground work so our dreams have strength?*

March 5

"Fears are learned, and if they are learned, they can be unlearned."   *-Karl Menninger*

Bobby, my boyfriend, had a wonderful nurse named Connie. who couldn't believe the miracle that came over him.

Modern science can only do so much and sometimes it takes an intervention of belief.

We are products of what we were taught to believe. It's no one's fault, it just is. If we can go forward, and let go of the past, all of our lives have hope. We were fed with good and bad information, so let's build on the good.

Connie told Bobby he's like a cat and then said, "What are you going to do with your other eight lives?"

How very precious life is. Isn't it worth some self discovery?

"For Today We'll Find A Way" *to have the courage to let go of some old fears. How many chances do we have?*

March 6

"Culture is the habit of being pleased with the best and knowing why."   -Henry VanDyke

How was business for you during the war in the Middle East? We went through a setback in January and February of 1991. Of course, people were generally worried and concerned.

We ran many specials at the time to generate some enthusiasm and let people see that if they look good, they'll feel better. Air travel was down because people were afraid to travel. We promoted a mini vacation to our salon.

When the going gets tough, the tough get going. Once we have made a commitment to our goals, we must find a way.

We're all lucky the war wasn't prolonged. Thanks to General Schwartzkopf who brought home VICTORY and our troops!

"For Today We'll Find A Way" to succeed one step at a time. Just do it!

March 7

"An investment in knowledge always pays the best interest."   *-Benjamin Franklin*

What separates the successful from the unsuccessful? Education is the answer!

I can remember the first seminar I went to 27 years ago. It cost $15. to learn the latest trend in haircutting. What an investment - I was hooked. I realized that to stay a cut above, education was a must. If you don't attend classes, the rest of the industry passes you up.

Our salon team looks forward to seminars. Setting new goals, developing a new game plan to achieve them and finally realizing our dream.

We are all capable of going to these programs. You say, "You can't afford it?" We say, "We can't afford not to go!" Our salon takes a little out of each check before an expensive seminar, so we don't have to pay for it all at once.

"For Today We'll Find A Way" *to attend some new seminars.*

March 8

"We can easily forgive a child who is afraid of the dark; the real tragedy of life is when adults are afraid of the light."   -*Plato (ca 400 BC)*

For me, being focused is the same as living in the light. Knowing each morning that somebody up there loves me, makes each day happier.

Sometimes when my day goes a little crazy, I take a few minutes and meditate. It clears my head and pulls things back together. It will also give you a boost of energy to carry on with your day.

When I reflect on my past, I really had much darkness in my life - not all darkness, but definitely some real gray areas.

When people come in to our salon, we get the same reaction, "This is such a friendly salon." We feel our light shines through - come visit us anytime.

"For Today We'll Find A Way" *for our human spirit to recover in the light.*

March 9

"One thing about heros, they are all committed and they all face tough times."   *-Rev. Robt. Schuller*

Do you have a hero? Someone you look up to with love and respect? Someone you know is always with you in spirit?

Arnie Miller is my hero. He has taught me that I can succeed and has given me the tools with which to do it.

As we go through life, sometimes we find false heros that lead us down some pretty lonely paths.

In my opinion, I was ready for change when I met the father of our industry, I only thank God I did. Step by step I am realizing the career of my dreams.

I have found a spiritual focus that has given me unconditional love and serenity.

Finding your own special focus will give you strength to bring out your own God-like qualities. We are all here to serve each other.

"For Today We'll Find A Way" *to synergize our way to being the best person we can be. Come fly with me.*

March 10

"Courage is very important. Like a muscle it is strengthened by use." -Ruth Gordon

A winner says, "Let's find out";
A loser says, "Nobody knows."
A winner makes commitments.
A loser makes promises.
A winner says, "I'm good, but not as good as I ought to be."
A loser says, "I'm not as bad as a lot of other people."
A winner credits his good luck for winning, even though it wasn't his good luck.
A loser blames his bad luck for losing, even though it wasn't his bad luck.
A winner listens.
A loser just waits until it's his turn to talk.
A winner respects those who are superior to him and tries to learn from them.
A loser resents the superiority of others and tries to find chinks in their armor.

"For Today We'll Find A Way" to be a winner!

March 11

"If I've learned one thing in life, it's in five years, today's problems won't matter." -Lar Park Lincoln

When I look back at all the years I wasted worrying about things that never materialized anyway, it really seems crazy. At the time, I did the best I could with the information I had.

Today I take one day at a time. When you focus yourself each morning and ask for spiritual guidance to carry you through your day, life is much easier.

It's nice to have a basic plan and goals set to achieve, then let go and let them happen. To try to control each moment will only lead to a life of frustration.

When I look at where I was five years ago, I am so thankful to be where I am today.

"For Today We'll Find A Way" *to live for today and make the right choices. Tomorrow will take care of itself.*

March 12

"As part of your God-given nature, you have the ability to love unconditionally and to experience unity with the world around you." -Harville Hendrix, Ph.D.

Life is so easy when we learn to live without a handicapped attitude. We are all created equal. My mother used to tell us you can achieve anything you set your mind to. She told us to live by one rule,. "We are no better than the next person and no one is better than us."

Let's all look to each other with love. How can we help the next person to help themselves? Do we look for the goodness in others? To be in sync with the world is a great feeling.

"For Today We'll Find A Way" *to look to the people that bring out the best in us. the ones that are dream builders. Today we will feel in sync with the universe.*

March 13

"It is not up to you to change your brother, but merely to accept him as he is."
-A Course in Miracles

Acceptance of one another is not an easy task. We all like people that are like us. Then we feel more accepting of ourselves.

When attending any 12-step meeting the saying goes, We are based on attraction not promotion. When people see the peace you have, they will want to find out how to get it.

Haven't you ever noticed when working with happy people you feel happier yourself? We have some pretty hectic days in our salon. When we pitch in and do it as a team, the day goes quickly and we feel good about our successes. We are all different and we all have good qualities and shortcomings. Why not concentrate on the positive?

"For Today We'll Find A Way" *to greet this day with acceptance of each other.*

March 14

"Courage is the price that life exacts for granting peace."   -Amelia Earhart

Haven't we all had a knot in our stomachs when a fussy client is getting color for the first time? How about a client with long hair changing her image for the first time? Our profession can be so emotional.

Our knowledge has a lot to do with each new service we encounter but we also have to figure in a person's personality. Having the courage to change a person's look is what our business is all about.

The sense of peace I feel when my client looks in the mirror and looks happy with her reflection is overwhelming.

"For Today We'll Find A Way" *to change many destinies. Let's go that extra mile and make our clients all that they can be.*

March 15

"Optimists not only interrupt their negative flow of thought and replace it with more logical assessments, they also try to see things in as favorable a light as possible." -Alan Lay McGinnis

I keep referring to Bobby's surgery for an aneurysm. All I have to offer is my life's experience and how to find your own personal focus. So "take what you like and leave the rest" (ala program, and my wonderful recovery).

Bobby had a nurse named Boonie, a pretty Chinese girl. (It's Boonie not Bonnie.) She told me at the height of his problems, "It doesn't look good, but I can pull him through," and she did. She knew inside it would be okay with a little luck.

From the moment we brought him to this hospital, I knew we were in the right place. I go with my gut feelings a lot, so far so good.

"For Today We'll Find A Way" *to understand what we think, we become.*

March 16

"Peace at any price doesn't give genuine peace. Genuine peace comes from making choices that create more life, not less."
            -Ernie Larsen and Carol Larsen Hegart

    The above quote comes from a favorite daily meditation book for adult children that I read with pleasure each morning, called *Days of Healing, Days of Joy*.

    I had the pleasure of attending a conference where Ernie Larsen presented. He has offered so many a way to find peace. It was listening to him that I realized if we were born into a family with dysfunction, it is no fault of our own. When there is a problem, there is always a solution.

    Their book is a favorite gift I give to people I care about. It sure is a nice way to start the day.

"For Today We'll Find A Way" *to make healthy choices for our own peace.*

March 17

"Life is God's novel. Let him write it."
-Isaac Bashevis Singer

To be spiritually guided is a way to find our own centeredness. To ask God for guidance each day makes life so much easier.

For me, every day is so precious because for the first time, I do feel life. My emotions are real and most of all my love of others reaches down to the depths of my soul.

There is so much to be positive about. Are we lucky enough to be healthy and able? Do we really drink in the beauty around us?

Last night I was coming home from a hair show in Milwaukee and I was exhausted. I looked up and the sun was going down and it looked orange and almost on fire. The clouds around looked like heaven right here on earth. It was refreshing. Now I ask you, don't we have a lot to be thankful for?

"For Today We'll Find A Way" *to be spiritually focused by asking God to guide us where we need to be.*

March 18

"Doing business without advertising is like winking at a girl in the dark. You know what you are doing but nobody else does."   *-Ed Howe*

To have a progressive salon you must advertise. It's so important to keep your name in the public eye. This isn't meant for just salon owners. Hairdressers can also advertise by sending post cards or handing out business cards attached to a sample of hair or skin care products.

I can afford to advertise in an area like Chicago only through the help of manufacturers. They co-op almost any kind of advertising from newspaper ads to billboards to give-away pens for your clients. Now I ask you, why can't you afford to advertise? It's an easy procedure even for those of us that don't like paper work.

"For Today We'll Find A Way" *to advertise. So let's start today. We will all be successful.*

March 19

"No one can change your life except for you; don't ever let anyone step all over you. Just open your heart and your mind. Is it really fair to feel this way inside?"   *-Wilson Phillips*

    Listening to this tape made me feel so good. Here we have three young talented people with careers of their own, who were raised by parents of the turbulent sixties. I was reading the words to the song on the inside of the tape. The female artists wrote on the bottom, "Thank God for giving us each other."

    Finding our spiritual focus can bring about great changes in our lives. In these times, we have so many options to choose. Recovery programs are free and every time I didn't feel like making a meeting I thought, "If I don't want to go, then I don't want to grow."

"For Today We'll Find A Way" to bring about great changes in our lives. Where are we spiritually?

March 20

"We are today the sum total of our experiences."
-Ali McGraw

Do you ever look back at a situation and say, "If I had only known then what I know now."

There is a reason we go through difficult times. We can sometimes seem to repeat the same bad times or bad relationships over and over. We need to learn, what it is we need to learn, so we can get on with our lives.

My love of our industry goes deep down into my soul. I work on a healthy life each and every day. When I was ready to grow, all the right teachers appeared to guide me. I couldn't be where I am today without all the helpful programs that our industry provides.

I thank my God each and every day for my business success and my personal well being.

"For Today We'll Find A Way" *to look at all of our life's experience with optimistic attitudes.*

March 21

"Two things that are a must to run a progressive salon are advertising and training."
-Duane Cole

We must train our people on the latest high touch high techniques and then advertise to show their expertise. This is an age of qualified professionals.

To sit in on a class of Duane's is a real experience. He seems to have his finger on the pulse of what our success is all about. He can make you understand and enjoy using the techniques to your best advantage and he makes it easy. He has good ideas like putting your new stylist by the door so clients can see the kind of work they do. Clients assume the new stylist will be in the last chair.

We have so many good people to educate us.

"For Today We'll Find A Way" *to do what we can do to help in training each other? Team work will help us all succeed.*

March 22

"What costs little is little worth." -Balasar Gracian

My friend Dave Delgato knows how to love and support us whenever we need it. His real name is Maher, but after watching Dave Delgato, the real estate mongol on late night TV, we nicknamed him Delgato. Our Dave, is a take charge person that gets the job done.

Dave is the one we call when the hot water tank goes cold or the air conditioning goes out or some minor inconvenience (ha-ha) takes place.

Don't you have an unsung hero that helps you when your salon falls apart or you have car trouble or house problems?

"For Today We'll Find A Way" to know that giving of oneself is the greatest gift of all. Do we always take the time to thank these special friends of ours?

March 23

"If a man does not keep pace with his companions, perhaps it is because he hears a different drummer."
　　　　　　　　-Henry David Thoreau

One day one of my dryers went out at the salon. I was kind of stuck because one was already broken and I needed both of them for the Friday morning rush.

The superintendent of our building is a good friend. Rich had his fourth anniversary in A.A. recently and his life is healthy now. He has also met a special lady, Barb, with whom to share his life.

He offered to take the dryers downtown to Veeco Manufacturer where I purchased them to get them fixed. My salesman George said they would do them right away. Well, our warranty was up by a few months, but they honored it. It didn't cost a thing, except a little help from a friend.

"For Today We'll Find A Way" *to help others. As Rich would say, "When you're living right, right things happen."*

March 24

"Stylists want to be appreciated. A simple thank you from the owner/management makes us feel good."
                              -Jeannie Carroll

I work with Jeannie and Kim. They are advisors and we work many shows together. They also work in the same salon.

It makes me feel so good to work with such bright young professionals. They are in their early twenties and already positive and very motivated. They dress so professionally, have wonderful attitudes, and are a great asset to the advisor team.

They both genuinely love this business as my team and I do. They are two young women you should meet at the next Midwest Show you attend.

"For Today We'll Find A Way" *to show that the love and support of our industry goes on and on and on and on...*

March 25

"Humor is a prelude to faith and language is the beginning of prayer."   *-Reinhold Niebuhr*

Bobby. my boyfriend, always teases me about having had a religious experience. I respond by saying that my life is focused spiritually.

After Bobby's brush with death (his aneurysm and subsequent neurosurgery) I'm sure he feels he's had a spiritual experience.

Through all the sickness and discomfort, he never lost his sense of humor. He joked and teased with everyone and made us laugh.

When he woke up the morning before his operation, I had Sister Ferdinand come up to pray for him. He smiled and said the Our Father with us. He's so special I took every precaution. I'm so thankful for my faith.

"For Today We'll Find A Way" *to bring humor and laughter to all the lives we touch today.*

March 26

"A loving world will be ours when we extend only love. That means the world does not have to change... The only thing that has to change is our attitude."   -Gerald Jampolsky

My sister, Fran is one of my role models. She gives love and a part of herself to all the lives she touches.

When I was twelve, I sent her picture in to Jim Lounsbury's Record Hop for Miss Teen Chicago. She was selected but declined to go. She said she would be embarrassed. Her inability to see her own beauty still amazes me.

Fran has such a strong sense of family. She and her husband Karl work with young couples preparing them for marriage. They also have five grown children and have been happily married for 30 years.

"For Today We'll Find A Way" *to give love and we will get love in return. Our attitude is loving!*

March 27

"If you have any faith, give me for heaven's sake, a share of it. Your doubts you may keep to yourself. I have plenty of my own."
                    -Johann Wolfgang von Goethe

My sister Mary is so very special to me. She has typed most of the pages of this affirmation book.

She has endured even with her disabilities of lupus and sjogrens diseases. She suffers considerably through no fault of her own.

The love and caring my sister shows me means so very much. When she gets down I tease her that she has to be well to type.

I have faith in my sister that she will continue to find a way to cope with these horrible diseases. I have faith in her spirit.

"For Today We'll Find A Way" *to share our faith by showing others the goodness we each have. Love and support will help everyone.*

March 28

"The hand that gives gathers."   *-English Proverb*

My whole family is in service related professions. Fran runs the service and office for Creative Mirrors. Deb is an oncology social worker. She helps patients and their families face cancer. Dennis is a DuPage County Sheriff and president of the Carol Stream baseball league. My sister Mary helps me with typing. My brother Rick, is an Itasca Policeman. The point is, we are all serving in one way or another.

It takes such special people to care for others. All of us in the beauty industry are in the service of making people look and feel good about themselves.

"For Today We'll Find A Way" *to be glad we all have so much love to give.*

March 29

"The first duty of love is to listen."   -Paul Tillich

I spent my morning with a dear friend and client. Her name is Fran Richards. She is the kind of person that brightens the room when she enters it.

Fran was diagnosed this week with lung cancer which has already spread to her bones. She is in her sixties. In the last three months, she has been going with a man named Sam. His late wife was Fran's friend. She died six years ago from cancer.

I spent the morning at the hospital doing her hair and nails. I listened to her fears and hopes. The most important thing is, she's not giving up. Her attitude is that she can beat it. She said having Sam in her life gives her the will to go on.

"For Today We'll Find A Way" to listen and extend love. We all need love and support.

March 30

"Example is not the main thing in influencing others. It is the only thing."   -Albert Schweitzer

How many positive messages come out of our mouths? If we listen fifteen minutes in the salon, what would we hear?

If we influence each other positively the outcome can be higher sales, better work conditions and most of all, better relationships within the salon.

How can we expect the stylists to be motivated and positive if the owner isn't?

Today, let's really listen to what we communicate in our messages. It has everything to do with our success.

"For Today We'll Find A Way" *to really listen to the messages we give. Let's learn to be positive.*

March 31

"When I came in they told me, let us love you until you can learn to love yourself."   -Anonymous

One of the issues I've had to deal with as an adult child of an alcoholic is abandonment.

My father called me one afternoon and said he was in Chicago (he lived in Florida). He asked me if I could meet him for dinner. I told him I was going to an ACOA meeting at 7:30 p.m. He asked if he could go along (his father was also an alcoholic).

As fate would have it, I was doing the lead on abandonment at my meeting. By the time the meeting started, my heart was racing and I had the hives. It was a good meeting and I introduced my dad. Some of our group knew him from A.A. when he lived in Chicago.

My dad died on December 26, 1989. He was in program for 29 years.

"For Today We'll Find A Way" *to face our fears head on so we can learn to love and respect ourselves.*

April 1

"We work to become, not to acquire."
                              -Elbert Hubbard

I will never forget the feeling of wonder that I felt the day my mother came home from the hair salon (my first memory around the age of 7). She looked so beautiful, her long hair done short and in the latest fashion.

My mind was made up, I would dedicate my life to making people look and feel beautiful. Each day I would dream of owning my own salon and making people feel special.

"For Today We'll Find A Way" *to accept that what our minds believe, we can achieve.*

April 2

"Judge a man by his questions rather than by his answers."   *-Voltaire*

   Will I be a great hair designer? Will I make my mark in the industry? Will I make a difference in my clients' lives? Will I bring my optimistic attitude to the people I touch each day? Will I bring color into their lives and bounce into their step?
   Our attitude is really up to us. Let's make the decision for a positive day and build our future together.

"For Today We'll Find A Way" *to treat each client with the enthusiasm we did on our first day.*

April 3

"If eyes were made for seeing, then beauty is its' own excuse for being."   *-Ralph Waldo Emerson*

Imagine wonder in a child's eyes, a smile from an elderly friend. It has been said that beauty is in the eye of the beholder. With that thought in mind, do you see the difference each of us can make as a salon professional?

Can you imagine what warmth a young stylist would feel when an established stylist looks over and says, "What a beautiful look! Can you show me how you did that?"

"For Today We'll Find A Way" *to look at another stylist's work and remember to look at it with love.*

April 4

"Whether you think you can or whether you think you can't, you are right." -Henry Ford

Is the glass half full or half empty? Is responsibility a privilege or a duty? Is the help we've been asked to give an opportunity or an obligation? Our attitude is everything! We can choose to have a good attitude or a bad attitude. Lucky for us the choice is all ours. Attitudes are ours alone.

What we practice, we become. If we practice looking at the bright side of each day, the sun will shine, no matter what the weather.

"For Today We'll Find A Way" *to give thanks today that our faith and gratitude will help us develop a good attitude.*

April 5

"He does not believe, that does not live by his belief."
                                    -Thomas Fuller

Have you ever heard the saying, "One day at a time/?" We try each day to keep focused and not overwhelm ourselves with the rest of our lives.

I read Al William's book, *All you can do, is all you can do, but all you can do is enough.* His personal goal is to go through 24 hours without a negative thought. Think of the power of that statement. Now, if I have a negative thought, that statement runs through my mind.

"For Today We'll Find A Way" *to tune into our surroundings and be thankful for what we have.*

April 6

"People with goals succeed because they know where they're going."   *-Earl Nightengale*

Have you ever felt that you were living in darkness? Not the gloom and doom darkness, not the darkness of night, but not living in divine order.

I used to hear the phrase "born again" and my feeling was that it sounded weird or that person must be different. I knew of no other way of explaining the different path my life has taken, but from the heart, I live with peace and harmony now.

"For Today We'll Find A Way" *to keep our focus and love unconditionally.*

April 7

"Choose the way of life. Choose the way of love. Choose the way of caring. Choose the way of goodness. It's up to you, it's your choice."
-Leo Buscaglia

I can remember the days before my first meeting with Dr. Lew. Sometimes when I'd see a client come through the door of my salon and I'd think, "Oh no, here she comes again, my day is ruined!" Now I honestly can say I love each and every person I encounter, in and out of the salon, because in understanding where they're coming from, I can choose to love them whether I agree with them or not.

Our work is better. Our caring and concern have shown that goodness makes for a better life.

"For Today We'll Find A Way" *to choose to love because it makes us feel good.*

April 8

"Honesty is the first chapter of the book of wisdom."
-Thomas Jefferson

Before finding my focus in life, I justified a lot of things. Maybe it was despair, a void and aloneness that is hard to explain, an emptiness that no amount of alcohol, people, work, or food could ever fill. I could be in a room full of people, and I felt like a square peg in a round hole. I would escape into my work and put on a mask so no one ever knew.

Through most of this, I was still optimistic and always searching to find a better way.

With a focus, I explore my feelings, and understand they don't make me good or bad, they just are.

"For Today We'll Find A Way" *to be honest with ourselves.*

April 9

"It is better to deserve honors and not have them, than to have them and not deserve them."
                                        -Mark Twain

Have you ever, as a stylist, taken credit for the success of a perm and style, as if there's no one else involved in the work I'm doing? Where would we all be without our assistant hanging over the bowl rinsing for five minutes, towel blotting and changing towels, getting ready for us to neutralize, then taking our client through more rinsing and finally pulling rods? Remembering that I started as an assistant, makes me realize never to forget where I started and keeps me honest.

"For Today We'll Find A Way" *to remember how team work makes for the ultimate salon experience.*

April 10

"Work joyfully and peacefully, knowing that right thoughts and right efforts will inevitably bring about the right results."   -James Allen

B.F. - before focus, I was into control, make it happen, demand things be done my way, so afraid to let go and let God guide me in the right direction. Sometimes I slip and try to take the controls and then I remember how it used to be, headaches, confusion, and a knot in my stomach. Life is simply easier now and much more joyful and peaceful, even after a long day at the salon, it's much more gratifying.

"For Today We'll Find A Way" *to let God grant us the serenity to accept the things we cannot change, the courage to change the things we can, and the wisdom to know the difference.*

April 11

"Each time you are honest and conduct yourself with honesty, a success force will drive you toward greater success. Each time you lie, even a little white lie, there are strong forces pushing you toward failure."   *-Joseph Sugarman*

    Success is certain. Because I have made the conscious decision to set my goals and realize that if there's a genuine honesty, a love greater than oneself will get us where we deserve to be.

"For Today We'll Find A Way" to know in our hearts, honesty really is the best policy.

April 12

"To measure the man measure his heart."
                    -Malcome S. Forbes

Have you felt a genuine empathy for the homeless? I've heard people say, "Well, why don't they get a job?' My heart really aches for people that don't have a roof over their heads or a pillow to lay down on. How about the comfort of a hot shower, a hot meal and the choice of how to spend their days and nights?

Don't you think the world would be a better place if we all tried to help?

"For Today We'll Find A Way" *to give a person with less than we have, some feeling of self worth and dignity.*

April 13

"If you would not be forgotten as soon as you are dead, either write things worth reading or do things worth writing."   -Benjamin Franklin

Have you ever heard that success is 1 percent inspiration and 99 percent perspiration? Good, hard work in our field will bring us success and fulfillment.

I'm sure each of us could tell a few client stories worth writing about, so listen to this.

My friend Lonnie who lives in a nursing home, came for a perm this morning. When I was helping her into the car to drive her back to the nursing home, she lost her footing and started to slip. I put my hands on her butt and started pushing her into the car. We both started laughing so hard and I couldn't stop and wet my pants. Lonnie said "I looked like a whore with my butt hanging out in public."

"For Today We'll Find A Way" *to see how lucky we are to make our clients laugh and forget their troubles for a few minutes.*

April 14

"If you judge people, you have no time to love them."   *-Mother Teresa*

We sometimes assume we really know what makes the next person tick. Each of us is so complex and have walked a different path to get to where we are today.

One evening, while having dinner with a colleague and friend, we were discussing the battle we both have with our weight. We both agreed that keeping extra weight on, was like a protective coating. She started to talk about therapy and said she was now in a healing process and shared that she had been sexually molested as a child beginning at age 5.

Sometimes, there are incidents that we bury so deep in our minds, that we aren't even conscious of them.

"For Today We'll Find A Way" *to love ourselves and others unconditionally.*

April 15

"Effort only fully releases its' reward after a person refuses to quit."   -Napoleon Hill

Those early years in the business were totally different than now. The "boss" took all the chemical work and we took the leftover or new clients. From that, we built our clientele. There was no advertising, it was word of mouth. Believe me, if you had a need to earn money, you got out and brought people into the salon. Reflecting on the old days, fear was always the motivation! It wasn't all bad in the days of $2 haircuts, $2.50 for a shampoo and set and complete perms for $10 to $15. But, there were many 12 hour days!

This important fact remains etched in my mind. With effort, I will grow each and every day!

"For Today We'll Find A Way" *to remember to treat everyone in the salon in a professional manner.*

April 16

"Treat people as if they were what they ought to be, and you help them to become what they are capable of being."   *-Boethe*

Encouragement! Where would we all be without it? Was your first boss encouraging? Mine was my idol. She had the most popular salon in our area. She had it all. Looks, a nice husband and son, and could she do hair! The most important thing is she believed in me. I wrote her a letter while I was living in LasVegas and thanked her for the start she gave me. She never answered, but I know mine was a first class action.

"For Today We'll Find A Way" *to reflect on our focus so we can be all that we want to be.*

April 17

"Progress not Perfection."   *-ACOA*

    Sometimes it's hard to remember life as a young stylist. Remember those days of uncertainty? Maybe the cut on your favorite client was too short. Remember the old rule, hair stretches 50% when wet. In those early days, 27 years ago, I wanted to please so badly. Well, thank God, I still have many of the clients with whom I started. In those early days, progress not perfection must have been their motto. I guess they could see the enthusiasm in my eyes. I can tell you I love each and every client dearly.

"For Today We'll Find A Way" *to help the young stylists in our lives. Never forget where we started.*

April 18

"A humble knowledge of oneself is a surer road to God, than a deep searching of the senses."
-Thomas A. Kempes

Through much soul searching, I've come to realize that the actions I dislike in someone else, are almost always what I fear in myself.

Reflect the next time someone goes against your grain, whether it be rudeness, poor attitude, being loud, self-righteous or judgmental. Are these the qualities we dislike most in ourselves?

"For Today We'll Find A Way" *to work towards finding good assets in others, no matter what their attitude is.*

April 19

"It's enthusiasm that will turn things around for you - real enthusiasm - the genuine article."
				-Dr. Albert E. Cliffe

Are you a dream builder? Lucky for me Arnie and his army are helping me to realize my dreams.

Do you ever have those days when your enthusiasm is a little low and you need a friend?

After my friend Bobby's neurosurgery, I was having a rough day. Even with all of my faith it's very hard to see someone you love going through being disoriented from having an aneurysm. I called Lynn Wright, Arnie's right hand, and she reassured me that Bobby would pull through. She said everyone is praying for him. If that isn't family, what is?

"For Today We'll Find A Way" to take on every day with enthusiasm.

April 20

"Somewhere along the line of development we discover what we really are, and then we make our real decision, for which we are responsible. Make that decision primarily for yourself, because you can never really live someone else's life, not even your own child's. The influence you exert is through your own life and what you become yourself."
-Eleanor Roosevelt

Have we all taken responsibility for paths our lives take? We can all make a difference if we choose to! As salon professionals, we can come together and make the world a better place.

"For Today We'll Find A Way" to take *responsibility for an optimistic day!*

April 21

"The empires of the future are empires of the mind."
-Winston Churchill

At a 7:00 a.m. breakfast meeting, Diana, a young assistant said, "I didn't want to get up this morning, but I decided to pretend I was a great hair designer and happily married and I was getting up to help support my family. I got ready quietly so I didn't wake my sleeping husband on a Saturday morning and set out for a positive day."

We all laughed and told Diana we were glad she shared her dream with us.

Good hairdressers are hard to find, so we encourage our assistants so we can promote from within.

"For Today We'll Find A Way" *to realize how hard our lives would be without team work!*

April 22

"Success is to be measured not so much by the position that one has reached in life, as by the obstacles which he has overcome while trying to succeed."   *-Booker T. Washington*

I've gone through some very strange obstacles in my life but there is a light at the end of the tunnel.

I'm lucky enough to have a wonderful daughter, Kelly and a loving son, Jamie. My life is truly blessed. As a single parent, my decisions weren't always the right ones, but overall I made more good decisions than bad. My life is getting better each and every day!

"For Today We'll Find A Way" to be thankful for our loved ones - truly the best asset anyone can wish for.

April 23

"Worry is a state of mind based on fear."
-Napoleon Hill

I overheard my salon manager talking to her mom. She said, "Mother, if you can prove to me that by worrying it will make things get better, then I'll sit down and worry with you. Until then, let's let it go and be happy."

The opposite of fear is courage, the courage to try to face our fears.

Worrying never accomplishes a thing except to discourage.

"For Today We'll Find A Way" *to take first class action for a positive day.*

April 24

"The worst loneliness is not to be comfortable with yourself."   *-Mark Twain*

I spent most of my life with a knot in my stomach. I lived through ulcers, gallbladder disease, nervous stomach, always striving for perfection.

I know today, that perfection for me is being comfortable with myself. I don't ever feel lonely anymore. A few years ago, I came to the realization that I have an excessive personality and I now have it work for me in a positive way.

I'm fortunate to have many young people in my life. If I can teach them anything, it's to see their own special goodness.

"For Today We'll Find A Way" *to tell people what makes them so special and unique.*

April 25

"All is well that ends well."   -John Heywood

If today was the last day of the world, what would be your life accomplishments?

Were you kind to the people you work with? Did you ever take the time to make an elderly person feel good?

How about being thankful for the guidance in your life, whether family, spiritual or helpful friends.

Why waste this wonderful day. Let's live each day like it was our last.

"For Today We'll Find A Way" *to treat every person with the kindness with which you like to be treated.*

April 26

"Fear is only an illusion. It is the illusion that creates the feeling of separateness, the false sense of isolation that exists only in your imagination."
-Jeroldine Saunders

In my first years as a stylist, we were all motivated by fear. The owner was "BOSS"! What she said was the law.

I remember our boss interviewing a young stylist named Marilyn. She said "Do you get sick?" Marilyn replied, "Not usually." The boss then countered, "You don't get sick in this business!" Talk about people skills. The boss continued, "Can you do hair?" Marilyn answered a shaky, "Yes." The boss said, "Be here tomorrow at 9:00 a.m., wear pink pants and a white uniform top." There was no dialogue. Could Marilyn buy the uniform? Did she have the money? The message was wear it or else.

"For Today We'll Find A Way" *to be motivated by courage and focus.*

April 27

"I can stand what I know, it's what I don't know that frightens me."   -Frances Newton

    Marilyn's first day... She came in at five minutes to 9. Our boss said, "Marilyn you're going to cut Pattie Green's hair." So Marilyn asked, "Where is my station?" The boss replied, "Opposite from me." So Marilyn took Pattie to the shampoo bowl and then over to her new station. She was never directed as to what product to use or how to work the bowl. Marilyn then asked the boss, "Do you have scissors?" She turned to Marilyn and said, "Didn't you bring them? How did you expect to cut hair, chew it off?"

    After work I schooled Marilyn on the ins and outs of life within the salon.

"For Today We'll Find A Way" *to succeed by working as a team.*

April 28

"They do not love who do not show their love."
-William Shakespeare

Shift our focus from being self-centered, to caring about other peoples' needs.

There is no room for love to flourish in the presence of obsession.

As I take responsibility for my own life, I am free to love others unconditionally.

I know in my heart some of the clients I work on each day, could get their hair styled just as well in another stylist's chair. They choose me because I care. When I hug them and say I love them, they know I mean it.

"For Today We'll Find A Way" *to reflect that we feel full of love; the emptiness is gone.*

April 29

"Most kids hear what you say, some kids do what you say, but all kids do what you do."
-Kathleen Casey Theisen

How about the old saying, "Do as I say, not as I do." The only way to have a healthy family is to break the chains of the past. I know we all do the best we can with what we know, so if we learn a better way to share with our families, won't each generation get stronger and healthier? What a way to find world peace, by starting with our own family unit, whether it's our work family or our family of origin.

So many lives are lived in excess - to be bigger, stronger, faster, better. How about concentrating on loving, caring, sharing, giving? Oh, what our children will learn!

"For Today We'll Find A Way" *to practice what we preach so we will have peace within our families.*

April 30

"One can never consent to creep when one feels an impulse to soar."   *-Helen Keller*

My boyfriend Bobby, my soul mate, died of a burst blood vessel when he was sleeping at home. He endured neurosurgery and a five week recovery at a rehabilitation hospital.

I wonder if his own personality figured into his inability to recover from his medical problems. He had an "I want it yesterday" attitude. He didn't know how to let go of controlling and be calm and allow the medical team to work unencumbered.

The only thing we really have control over is ourselves and our attitude. Once we learn that, life can be so much sweeter. We can guide, we can suggest, but it is up to others what path they take.

"For Today We'll Find A Way" *to focus and guide our energies to develop our own inner strength and make the right choices.*

May 1

"Imagine the Super Bowl without any goal lines, or an airplane in midair without a destination. When we lack a goal, we are aimlessly in the air without the power of purpose."   -Dr. Lew Losoncy

We can achieve so much more by setting realistic goals for ourselves.

As a young stylist, doing a perm was an all day affair. Our goal then was to do a great job and make the client proud to hold her head up and say who her hairdresser was. Goals can be fun and easy. First class action is to suggest a perm, color or any other service from which our client might benefit. You'll be amazed what a simple suggestion can do.

"For Today We'll Find A Way" *to look over your client list and see what new service will benefit the client.*

May 2

"Nothing great was ever achieved without enthusiasm."   -Ralph Waldo Emerson

I can remember how fearful I was cutting my friends' hair in junior high.

My mom would yell out the back door, "I can't believe you kids are letting her cut your hair!" I would reassure them enthusiastically that I knew what I was doing. Somehow I always pulled it off. The old "fake it till you make it theory!" I knew I had a special gift.

"For Today We'll Find A Way" *to greet the day with enthusiasm and be thankful for the life we have.*

May 3

"Tell me what company you keep, and I'll tell you who you are."   -Cervantes

As a stylist, aren't some of your best moments sharing something with another stylist that only we would understand? It's kind of a universal foreign language hairdressers have with each other.

How about natural base level on a color? How about the five C's: cut, curl, color, condition and client satisfaction? Volume options: 10, 20, 30 and 40 volume.

"For Today We'll Find A Way" *to share with our fellow professionals, in an out of the salon, to make all of our days better.*

May 4

"Let us run with patience the race that is set before us."   *-Hebrews 12:1*

We all know the effects of impatience, a lost client, bad results on a color or perm, losing our temper with another stylist.

Patience is a tool that helps every day you spend in the salon. Show caring, to your clients and fellow co-workers. Believe that being patient with one another will give everyone who goes through the salon a sense of well being, a family spirit within the salon.

"For Today We'll Find A Way" *to ask for the spiritual guidance to help us all to be patient with each other.*

May 5

"Never make the mistake of limiting the visions of your future by something as narrow as the experiences of your past."   -Dr. Jonas Salk

Ten years ago, I was lucky enough to have my sales consultant, Joel, come to me and say, "Colleen, I want you to meet someone at the Midwest Show. He's developed a new company and I really think he will make the difference in the beauty industry." Joel has always been very supportive of me. He had asked me to listen to a new manufacturer, so we kept the appointment. That day totally changed my life. I'm listening to this fellow professional and his wife, I heard and felt the enthusiasm he felt for our industry. I felt he would realize his dream. This was my first, of many, experiences with Arnie and Sydell Miller - true visionaries of our industry.

"For Today We'll Find A Way" *to be glad we take positive action to better the salon.*

May 6

"If High Tech is a key that opens doors to your future. High Tech, High Touch is the Master Key that will open all the doors to your future."
                              -Dr. Lew Losoncy

Have you ever had a day when no matter how hard you tried, it seemed that your work wasn't as good as it usually is? As Certified Salon Professionals, we know we've all had those days. Did our clientele leave us never to return? No, because they could see it bothered us, more than it did most of them. Most of the Salon Professionals I know are perfectionists. Why do our clients love us and don't want anyone else to do their hair? Is it "High Tech?" Not on your life. It is "High Touch" all the way. There's a lot of great hair designers, but my clients know I care, as yours do too!

"For Today We'll Find A Way" *to remember to thank our clients for supporting us.*

May 7

"A new world is simply a new mind."
-Marilyn Ferguson

After meeting Arnie and Sydell Miller, I was so impressed with the genuineness of who they are.

I went back to my salon and sent back the two product lines that I was currently carrying and ordered their line.

My feeling on having one complete line, is that there's less confusion. It's easier for our team to learn one complete line and use it effectively.

The exception to the one line theory is, that if you're in a big mall, multiple lines are a good idea.

I believe in Arnie and Sydell's philosophy. I can't explain it exactly. I just knew in my heart that I could count on these two loving people. For me, this was the catalyst that turned my life around.

"For Today We'll Find A Way" to find our new world!

May 8

"Only the human being is capable of changing his outer world by a simple change of his inner world."
-William James

I can remember the excitement I felt going into the salon and telling each client about our new line, and how Arnie wanted to have a line exclusively created for hairdressers by hairdressers. I know my stylists were a little afraid, but they trusted me and felt the enthusiasm I did. The past ten years have revolutionized our salon. I remember calling the hotline one evening about a perm client and you guessed it! At 7:00 p.m. Chicago time, 8:00 p.m. Cleveland time, Arnie answered the hotline and answered my questions. That's the support I've always felt.

"For Today We'll Find A Way" *to accept that change is growth. Be happy for all change. As one door closes, a new door opens.*

May 9

"The hairstylist is actually the number one mental health agent in the community."   -Dr. Lew Losoncy

Have you ever had a client that sat in your chair, with big tears rolling down her cheeks, because she just lost her husband and feared being alone? In many cases, you were the first person she thought of to pull her together. I know that when my dear client Helen sat in my chair, all I could do was hug her. I felt so sad for her. Since that day, we are very close and there have been lots more hugs and a bond that only we, as salon professionals, could understand.

"For Today We'll Find A Way" *to strive for unconditional love with everyone we encounter today.*

May 10

"What draws a client to her hairdresser? According to one survey two out of three people choose their stylist by their social abilities, not their hair cutting skills."   *-Wall Street Journal*

    I've had this conversation with every young stylist I've ever had the pleasure of working with. "The reason my clients come to me is not because I do their hair better than the next stylist. It's because they like me as a person." There are many good stylists but the client will stay in our salon year after year because they feel a part of our salon family. I also share with my stylists. Any client they can move to their book is 100% fine with me. It makes me feel good to have our salon clients feel comfortable changing stylists. Positive people skills are as important as learning to use your shears.

"For Today We'll Find A Way" *to reflect on why each client picked you to be their stylist.*

May 11

"Do not forget the most important fact that not heredity and not environment are determining factors. Both are giving only the frame and the influences which are answered by the individual in regard to his styled creative power."
                              -Alfred Adler

Don't you often wonder why certain people's lives cross our lives? Divine order to me, means a lot. In those years, I thought I could control what happened in my life totally, I would have never understood divine order at all. Now, I let go and let God. My spiritual life is my total focus, then family and then my career. It's a matter of priorities.

"For Today We'll Find A Way" *to let God grant us the serenity to accept the things we cannot change, the courage to change the things we can and the wisdom to know the difference.*

May 12

"The first person in a conversation to draw a breath shall be the listener."   -Mark Twain

Do we really listen to our clients? How good is a haircut or a perm, if it's not what they want?

If we take the time to do an effective consultation, doesn't it make our job much easier?

Being a good listener in our profession can really determine the success or failure of retaining our clientele.

"For Today We'll Find A Way" *to remember how fragile a client's feelings are, so try and hear what they're not saying.*

May 13

"Only passions, great passions, can elevate the soul to great things."   *-Dennis Diderot*

We all have great passion for our work, for only the strong survive. How do we get strong? Education!! How many classes have we all attended?

If every class gives us just one good idea to make our life in the salon easier, isn't it worth it? Commitment is every professional's way to success.

Do doctors hesitate to better their knowledge?

"For Today We'll Find A Way" *to make a commitment to grow as a professional.*

May 14

"Prayer should be the key of the day and the lock of the night."   *-Thomas Fuller*

Do we start out each morning thankful for the day? I have learned to set my own mood by reading affirmation books. A quiet time each morning can be so refreshing. Getting in touch with our own spirituality can really give us serenity and peace.

My belief in a higher power is what my world is all about. When my day is ended, I feel such a security in knowing my God loves me and has been with me throughout the day.

"For Today We'll Find A Way" *to be thankful for our spiritual guidance.*

May 15

"Love is an art of endless forgiveness, a tender look which becomes a habit."   -Peter Ustinov

Sometimes a love can come into your life and touch you in a very special way and you both know your lives are better for it.

Bob Walker was a special love to me. We had four months of fun. We talked on the phone ten times a day and spent almost every evening together. We had a wonderful Christmas dinner together that Bob cooked for 48 guests. Our families spent a special holiday together.

I loved his children, Bob Jr., Cheryl and Ben, from the first moment. He also loved Kelly and Jamie on first contact. As they say, it's better to have loved and lost, than never to have loved at all.

Bobby came home from the hospital and the third night went to sleep and another aneurysm burst. Faith will sustain me and he will be missed.

"For Today We'll Find A Way" *to look at each other tenderly so our live is all forgiving.*

May 16

"You can't get $100. for a perm if you look like you need $100."   *-David Bagwell*

The magic is **You**. A picture is worth a thousand words! Would you feel confident if you went to a doctor and they came in to examine you dressed for a trip to the beach? How we dress tells our clients, new and old, what to expect. Did you ever notice how much better your day goes when you are dressed as a salon professional, hair done in a current style, makeup, clothes cleaned and pressed, shoes polished, hose on? A common sense approach can make the difference in the respect our clients have for us.

How we dress outside the salon can reflect our personality or where we're going. To sell beauty we must look good, for all age groups, not just our own.

"For Today We'll Find A Way" *to look as well as we can and dress as a professional.*

May 17

"Success is never final and failure is never fatal; it's courage that counts."   *-Unknown*

When we talk to young stylists, do we encourage them?

A young stylist that watches your every move only needs positive affirmation from us, the established stylist. Everything looks easy when you are good at it.

What I find so great about my life as a stylist is we can all learn together. When we sit in a class together, we all see things a little differently. When we put into action what we've learned, we see the creativity that is essential to succeed.

I guess we all should be thankful hair grows because no matter how good *we* think we are, if we kept every client, we wouldn't need to grow.

"For Today We'll Find A Way" *to take the time to treat each client as if they were our only one.*

May 18

"We should not let our fears hold us back from pursuing our hopes."   *-John F. Kennedy*

Do you remember the fear you had going from beauty school to working in a salon where people were paying top dollar for your services?

We can all recall the nervous feelings we went through in those early days. We can all have compassion for the young stylist. If we just think back and try and put ourselves in their shoes, we can set our egos aside and welcome them with open arms and a hug.

"For Today We'll Find A Way" *to remember where we've been so we can appreciate where we are going.*

May 19

"The process of changing a life style is more important than reaching a goal or measuring a performance."   -Theodore Isaac Rubin

Oh, the changes I've been through in my career! I've had two marriages, two wonderful children, two stormy divorces, and many personal changes. I've done a lot of searching to find my own serenity.

I came from an alcoholic home and I'm so thankful I found my way to Adult Children Anonymous. I have all the characteristics of an excessive personality, and now I no longer abuse alcohol. I live one day at a time and I no longer have a knot in my stomach, or ulcers or frustration. I've also learned acceptance and not to be so judgmental of others.

"For Today We'll Find A Way" *to look for the good in others and be thankful for the peace we have found.*

May 20

"I have never let my schooling interfere with my education."   *-Mark Twain*

On this journey of life there is so much to learn about each other.

We can be the only bright spot in another person's growth.

As I sat in the little church at Bob's funeral, I reflected on the fun we had together and how our children were a big part of what love we found in each other. Bobby Jr. came over to me crying and hugged me. After shedding lots of tears together he said, "Colleen, you'll never know how much you've helped me and made me feel good about myself. I love you so much."

Our strength is in our young. Why not encourage rather than discourage them?

"For Today We'll Find A Way" *to open our hearts and get an education on life.*

May 21

"Health and cheerfulness naturally beget each other."   *-Joseph Addison*

I have a client that goes through periods of depression. During these times she gets physically sick with all kinds of ailments and is also unhappy with everything, including her hair.

When she's feeling good about herself, she loves her hair. When she's depressed, she doesn't like her hair and complains that her hair didn't stay.

I've learned through taking Dr. Lew's psychology classes, not to take her reactions personally, because she's upset with herself, not with me. We also learned how to bring our clients around to feeling more positive.

"For Today We'll Find A Way" *because good health and happiness go hand in hand.*

May 22

"There are as many ways to live and grow, as there are people. Our own ways are the only ways that should matter to us."   -Evelyn Mandel

As we try to better ourselves, by working through the past and moving towards our own personal growth to be the best that we as an individual can be, we are not in a race with anyone but ourselves.

We are all here to accomplish what we were sent here to do.

A very wise old friend told me, "We are all where we are, because that's where we need to be."

Let's not try to run anyone else's race but our own.

"For Today We'll Find A Way" *to look into our own personal growth.*

May 23

"A complete re-evaluation takes place in your physical and mental being when you've laughed and had some fun." -Catherine Ponder

Part of being a good hairdresser is being able to make people laugh. I've often been told I should have been a comedian, but I've got the best of both worlds.

It really warms my heart to see people laugh. There is so much sadness in the world, that it's important for your clients to sit in your chair, and be able to escape their problems for a little while.

"For Today We'll Find A Way" *to make our clients laugh and have some fun today.*

May 24

"Is not fear the only attitude that ever stops us? Is not courage the antidote to fear? And is it not encouragement that brings out the courage to overwhelm the fear?" -Dr. Lew Losoncy

Do you remember the first haircut you gave in beauty school? I had the cold sweats. Such fear until my teacher, Miss Ann, came by with a word of encouragement. She said to my client, "You'll love your hair. Colleen is one of our best students!" Well, you guessed it! I had the confidence to go on. I don't think my client knew I was a new student until I put her under the dryer with her cape on. As she started to perspire, I went over and said, "No extra charge for the steam bath." All the other students laughed with me.

"For Today We'll Find A Way" *to see it is healthy to be able to laugh at ourselves.*

May 25

"Strong hope is a much greater stimulant of life than any single realized joy could be."
                        -Friedrich Nietzsche

    In this era, families have to deal with divorce, dysfunction, drug abuse, alcohol abuse, teen pregnancies, single parent homes, illness and unhappiness and the heartaches these can bring.

    In these days of despair that have hit most families in one way or another, what have we got? HOPE!

    The only way to change the world is for each of us to do our part.

"For Today We'll Find A Way" to bring hope to all the paths that cross ours.

May 26

"The great good God looked down and smiled and counted each his loving child, for Monk and Brahmin, Turk and Jew, loved him through the Gods they knew."   *-Alfred Lord Tennyson*

    I have so many friends of different faiths. Having a great understanding of each other, and knowing a power greater than ourselves, can lead us to a life of sanity.

    As we go through life, if we feel scattered, we must concentrate our efforts on being centered. Seeing the whole picture can insure finding our centeredness.

"For Today We'll Find A Way" *to respect everyone's spiritual journey.*

May 27

"Thank God every morning when you get up, that you have something to do which must be done, whether you like it or not."   -Charles Kingsley

Do you take on the events of your life with enthusiasm, or do you moan about the daily routine? Being a spectator, rather than a participator, is the result of the age of automation.

Being needed is wonderful. Elderly people in an old age home must feel despair, if they no longer feel needed.

My friend Lonnie (age 86) says, "I wish I could give you as much as you give to me." At 86, she doesn't realize how much more she gives me than I give her.

"For Today We'll Find A Way" *to contact an elderly friend, just so we can both feel good.*

May 28

"The art of being wise is the art of knowing what to overlook."   *-William James*

    We have all worked with stylists that think the world revolves around them. They act as if, without their expertise, the industry would never make it.

    This kind of stylist doesn't recognize the actions of a true professional and all the benefits of team work. It could also be, that they haven't had enough humbling experiences behind the chair. For me, I feel empathy for someone that is so wrapped up in themselves. I'm a firm believer that everyone is where they are, because that's where they need to be.

"For Today We'll Find A Way" *to remember sometimes the wise thing to do is overlook someone's shortcomings.*

May 29

"Being entirely honest with oneself is a good exercise."   -Sigmund Freud

We have all had to debate honesty more than once in our lives.

One form of honesty for me has been writing this affirmation book. I hope if one person can gather momentum to be honest with themself, it will be worthwhile.

None of us have to be ashamed of what life has dealt us. Be thankful and go forward. No one's family has a "Leave it to Beaver" lifestyle, so let's find strength in the positives and grow each day.

"For Today We'll Find A Way" *because self honesty makes us feel good about ourselves.*

May 30

"Courage is rightly esteemed the first of all human qualities because courage is the quality that guarantees all other qualities." -Winston Churchill

Do any of you remember the old tint machines of the late 60's?

In the first salon I worked in, we had a client that passed out while under the tint machine. I heard her head clunk, and I instantly thought she was dead! I turned to my boss and said, "What will we do with her body?" I guess I thought if I could get rid of the evidence, all would be okay.

Well, the paramedics arrived and they wanted to take her to the hospital with tint on, and I said, No way." As I started rinsing out the tint, she regained consciousness.

"For Today We'll Find A Way" *to see that when it seems like a catastrophe, it is only an inconvenience.*

May 31

"An ounce of encouragement is worth a pound of praise."   -Dr. Lew Losoncy

In our salon, we have an instinctive stylist named Cari. She has such a knack for seeing another stylist, myself included, struggling with someone's hair. She'll inevitably say, "What a great style, you look so good!"

No matter how many years you've been styling hair, once in awhile you'll get someone that is impossible to please, or her hair just doesn't do what you want it to do.

If we all encourage each other on, aren't our days in the salon much easier?

"For Today We'll Find A Way" *to remember there is a thoughtful Cari in all of us.*

June 1

"If we find nothing of interest where we are, we are likely to find little of lasting interest where we wish to go."   *-Edwin Way Teale*

Do we tune into our surroundings each day? Do we set our daily goals?

There was a time in my life when I would drag myself into the salon, wondering how I would have the energy to make it. The days of depression are now gone for me. If I have a bad day, that's just what it is, a bad day. Not a bad week, or a bad year, or a bad life. I'm so thankful for the growing in my life. My spiritual life has given me focus.

"For Today We'll Find A Way" *to have an interesting day by really tuning into our surroundings.*

June 2

"A friend is a person with whom I may be sincere. Before him I may think aloud."
-Ralph Waldo Emerson

How many fellow professionals can you trust to be sincere? It takes a lot of trust to confide in someone. I'm a very open person and I have found a lot of genuine friends that I can trust.

Once in awhile, we might be disappointed by telling someone something and hearing it later, in the form of gossip. Too bad that the person was so hollow inside, as to not keep your conversation confidential.

The law of averages - I've found more people I could trust, than people I couldn't trust.

"For Today We'll Find A Way" *to have a friend, we have to be a friend.*

June 3

"In dealing with other people, remember the three C's: you didn't cause it, you can't control it and you can't cure it."   -Lorna P.

As a child we learn our ways from our parents. I was lucky enough to have a wonderful mother and two great brothers and four loving sisters. Our father was an alcoholic and for many years I buried the memories of those dysfunctional years. Now, I look back and understand certain characteristics I have and why! I've always searched, knowing in my heart, there's a better way. I've let go of the past and I look forward to a better life each day.

"For Today We'll Find A Way" and peace will be with you.

June 4

"Fate chooses our relatives; we choose our friends."
-Jacques Bossuet

None of us need be without a healthy family. Real families are made up of people that love us, unconditionally, whether they are relatives or not. The healthy, whole American family system can be found not only in our family of origin, but also in our professional family.

Over the years, I have worked with many different product lines, and for me, that family feeling came when I was first introduced to Arnie and Sydell Miller. It's hard to explain unless you are already involved with them. Team spirit is always there. Family support is as close as the phone.

"For Today We'll Find A Way" *to be thankful for our family of origin and our chosen professional family.*

June 5

"Many strokes overthrow the tallest oaks."
                              -John Lyley

Long journeys are made one step at a time. Nothing is impossible if we set our minds to it!

You might say, "But I'm young and have no money. How will I ever afford a hair salon?" Well, this is one Irish girl that can tell you, if there's a will, there's a way!

My first salon was about 200 square feet; but it was mine and I loved it. Two stylist chairs, four dryers, two shampoo bowls and I was in business! When I would drive by, I would look at this little salon with love. It was a beginning.

"For Today We'll Find A Way" *to focus everyday, in every way so we are one step closer to our goals!*

June 6

"Only God can fully know what absolute honesty is. Therefore, each of us has to conceive what this great ideal may be, to the best of our ability."
                                       -Bill W.

Have you ever self-actualized? We can all do a lot of soul searching, and as we grow, remember it's hard to be there, if we're still here.

Setting our spiritual goals is important for inner peace. Many people confuse being wealthy with peace. There's a lot of people, that have lots of money, and still have no inner peace.

We can all find spiritual guidance, no matter what religion we are, by sharing what we have, our sense of peace with others.

"For Today We'll Find A Way" *to take some quiet time and ask for guidance. It only takes a few minutes, and it's a feeling that lasts all day.*

June 7

"Nothing is to be had for nothing."   -Epictetus

My cousin, Dan, has helped me to work smart, not hard. He is the kind of person everyone loves. He gives of himself, and he can guide others to bring out their own potential. Rather than to do the work for someone, the feeling of watching others grow is so very gratifying.

Do we take the time to show young stylists our ways, or do they have to try and pick it up on their own?

Being a visual person, I'm lucky to be able to watch another artist and pick up what they're doing.

"For Today We'll Find A Way" *to share our knowledge with other professionals, makes us feel better than it does them.*

June 8

"Most people ask for happiness on condition. Happiness can only be felt if you don't set any conditions."   -Arthur Rubinstein

When my son Jamie was very young, I used to try to control his every move. My motivation was to help him avoid all the pitfalls I had fallen into.

I'm so thankful I've learned to let go. He was nineteen before I realized the two most important things we can give any young person, whether it be our own child or a young person we work with, are roots and wings.

Don't we all feel the happiest when we love unconditionally?

"For Today We'll Find A Way" to love the Jamie's in our lives without controlling.

June 9

"SUCCESS is many things to many people. If you have the courage to be true to yourself, live up to your potential, be fair with others and always look for the good in any situation, then you will have been the best that you can be and there's no greater success than that."   *-Linda Lee Elrod*

I received this message on a cup from my friend and client, Bev Bohannon, for my 43rd birthday. She said, "I saw it and it reminded me of you."

I couldn't have been paid a bigger compliment!

"For Today We'll Find A Way" *to focus on our own successes to make us the best that we can be.*

June 10

"He has the right to criticize who has the heart to help."   *-Abraham Lincoln*

My daughter Kelly, believe me, is every mother's dream! She used to say, "Mom, I'll never be like you." I guess in my dysfunctional days she wanted me to know there's a better way. Today, Kelly works beside me, a great professional. She's also in college. She wants to work with children someday because she has a way of seeing a good child in all children. Kelly can take a child that seems impossible, and talk and laugh them through cutting their hair. All children love her as she loves them.

"For Today We'll Find A Way" *to remember the children of today are the clients of tomorrow.*

June 11

"The man who never alters his opinion, is like standing water and breeds reptiles of the mind."
  -William Blake

Sharing this affirmation book with you has helped me find the truth within myself and helps give me a peaceful heart.

A dear friend of mine, Carole Lyden Smith, and I, were talking at the Midwest Beauty Show in 1990. I said, "I'd really like to write an affirmation book for hairdressers, but I haven't had any formal training in writing."

She said, "Write from your heart and you will never go wrong."

"For Today We'll Find A Way" *to remember there's a good book in all of us.*

June 12

"In a crisis, the rich are as helpless as the poor."
-Anonymous

Haven't we all had a wealthy client that was in despair? No matter what economic existence we have, we are all just people. When there are problems with health, family and business, money doesn't mean the heartache stops. Money is a measure of one's labor, but it is only a vehicle to help us do things we want to do in our lifetime.

How much do we help others by sharing what we have? Do we create careers? Do we create a family for those that are estranged from their biological family?

"For Today We'll Find A Way" to understand, rich or poor, we are all on a journey that *we can't make alone.*

June 13

"The truth will set you free, but first it will make you miserable."   *-Garfield*

When working on certain issues in our lives, sometimes it has to hurt before it gets better.

When I was young and through most of my adulthood, I was afraid of being alone. Have you ever felt alone in a crowded room? I have learned to face my problems rather than run from them or drown them. In all honesty, I never feel alone anymore.

Inner peace or serenity is what happiness is all about. Security is in knowing spiritual focus.

Have you ever had the notion, that buying this house or that car will make me happy. Has instant gratification ever given you true happiness?

"For Today We'll Find A Way" *to be thankful that there's always help available to better our lives.*

June 14

"My best high was never as good as my worst day sober."   *-Don Johnson*

In the days that I tried to escape by binge drinking, I looked for peace in the immediate gratification of life in the fast lane. I couldn't explain it any better than Don Johnson did. So many people chase an escape high, when serenity is life's best high imaginable.

My old friends think I'm weird and that I found religion. All I have discovered is my own spirituality. If I choose to go to the church of my choice, great! If I choose not to, that's also an individual's own choice.

"For Today We'll Find A Way" to be thankful that we can find our own recovery and look forward to a life of love and peace.

June 15

"Loneliness expresses the pain of being alone and solitude expresses the glory of being alone."
                    -Paul Tillish

The highway of recovery is, as Ernie Larson and Carol Larsen Hegarty express in *Days of Healing, Days of Joy,* the road that runs between loneliness and solitude.

It's not to say we all need a recovery program, but if we choose to grow on our journey of life, growth is a recovering all on it's own.

Enjoy the solitude in your life. Don't be afraid of the quiet moments, because when you look back, you'll learn to treasure where you are now.

"For Today We'll Find A Way" *to recognize that we are all growing through our journey in life.*

June 16

"All the knowledge that I possess, everyone else can acquire, but my heart is all my own."
  -Johann Wolfgang Von Hoethe

Each young stylist that comes into my life is so very special. I choose to share all my experiences with all that care to learn. I know in my heart, that each person I've had the pleasure of working with, was sent especially to me, so that we can learn from each other.

We have a new team member in our salon. Her name is Stacey. She comes in each day with such enthusiasm in her eyes. She has long, natural curly blond hair and an infectious smile that would warm your heart. I knew in my heart, on her first day, that she would go the distance.

"For Today We'll Find A Way" *to see the SPECIALNESS in all our coworkers*

June 17

"Laugh and be well."   *-Matthew Green*

Have you ever heard that people have been cured through laughter?

We can all make life a lot easier by laughter.

My sister Deb is an oncology social worker. Her career is to help patients and their families through the devastation of cancer. She keeps such a positive attitude and caring way to help these people in their time of need.

Through education, she and her partner Susan reduce the fears patients and families have and guide them through life changes that are devastating when they don't know what to expect.

She told me that they all cry from time to time, but also find that laughter is good for the soul.

"For Today We'll Find A Way" *to bring laughter to another person is a day well spent.*

June 18

"Not everyone that is faced can be changed, but nothing can be changed until it's faced."
  -James Baldwin

For years, I buried the hurt that growing up without a father caused. I was angry, confused and felt abandoned.

I couldn't change the fact that he was an alcoholic, but now that I have faced the hurts, the pain has gone away.

I know now, that to have a healthy family life, the people in the family have to be healthy.

If for no other reason, we have to make a better way for our children and grandchildren.

I'm here to tell you, finding your own serenity is possible and wonderful.

"For Today We'll Find A Way" *for our spiritual focus will bring us serenity, by letting go and letting it happen.*

June 19

"He who is being carried, does not realize how far the town is."   *-Nigerian Proverb*

Sometimes we go through life trying to protect those around us, when it is better for them to go through the rough times themselves.

As a mother, I thought I could protect my children from the hurts of the world. The older I get, I know I am here to support them through the rough times, but can't take the pain for them. We can't shield our loved ones from feeling. To mask bad feelings is truly unjust.

We all have to go through some pain in our lives. It's what brings us to where we are.

"For Today We'll Find A Way" *to recognize our feelings and realize that it is a big part of growing healthy within.*

June 20

"That is the happiest conversation where there is no competition, no vanity, but a calm, quiet interchange of sentiments."   *-Samuel Johnson*

One of the nicest dinners I've ever shared was with my friend, Carol Lyden Smith and my daughter Kelly.

Carol told us about her granddaughter's birth and how wonderful it was.

We shared old experiences and things about our lives that made the evening so very special for all of us. Three hairdressers exchanging sentiments. I guess it's what you'd call "female bonding", and it will be an evening I will always treasure in my heart.

"For Today We'll Find A Way" *to show we are thankful for all the dear friends we make on our journey through life.*

June 21

"I myself believe that the evidence for God lies primarily in inner personal experiences."
                                    -William James

The longest day of the year...will always bring mixed emotions for me. My sister Carrie, was killed in a car accident on this day. Please understand, it has taken me many years to be able to let go of my grieving, but it is true, time does heal all wounds.

I know when you have belief in a higher power, that through his guidance, we learn that it isn't up to us to question.

I used to say, "I know how you feel," when someone died, but until you live through it, you have no idea. Our God be with us all.

"For Today We'll Find A Way" *to try and remember each and every day, we don't know the load our clients and fellow workers carry. Try and give unconditional love and it will come back to you.*

June 22

"If you hate a person, you hate something in him that is a part of yourself. What isn't part of ourselves doesn't disturb us."   -Hermann Hesse

Haven't we all known people whose personalities clash with ours? Do you wonder just what makes us feel this way?

Through a lot of soul searching and salon psychology programs, I have discovered a new me. Do you know why? I see people through different eyes now. When we understand where others are coming from, it's so much easier to like them. I guess liking myself better helps too!

"For Today We'll Find A Way" *to look at people with a new compassion and understanding.*

June 23

"Patience is the best remedy for every trouble."
-Platuers

Our world is so fast paced. Immediate gratification is the order of the day. Everyone seems to want a quick fix - a hurry up and wait society. Get it done no matter what kind of a job we perform.

When we come back to reality, we understand what all of these things have caused. We are now concerned for our environment, and trying to get back to basics. We have to each do our part to make it work.

Patience and harmony, are something I think we all want, but it has to start with us!

"For Today We'll Find A Way" *to show our patience so we will have a positive productive day.*

June 24

"Where there is an open mind, there will always be a frontier."   *-Charles F. Kettering*

As we grow on our journey through life, let's take a fresh look each day.

We can choose to say life is boring, but life is only boring to boring people

We can choose to look at the beauty we have all around us. The sun shining, the trees growing and beautiful, fresh flowers.

We get fresh flowers each week in our salons, because it makes not only our clients feel good, but us too. It also helps us network with the flower shop down the street. That's what success is all about, helping each other grow!

"For Today We'll Find A Way" *to really tune in and find what's right with the world.*

June 25

"Quality is not an act. It is a habit."   *-Aristotle*

Do you greet your first client with, "You must be my 9 o'clock" or do you check your appointment book and greet her with, "Good morning Mrs. LaVezzie, how are you today?" Which would be the first class action? Everyone likes to feel important.

Have you ever noticed a stylist really fuss over a client because they were prominent? I feel if everyone is paying the same price, they all deserve the same service.

Service is the key to a busy salon. Aren't we all in the process of becoming the best that we can be?

"For Today We'll Find A Way" *to form good habits that lead to quality work.*

June 26

"Quality shows not only the ability to persist, but in the ability to start over."   -F. Scott Fitzgerald

Some nights when I lock the salon, I think I can't do another head of hair. Then I go home, get some rest and wake up the next morning ready to make everyone I see, look the best they can. After 27 years, I still love what I do!

We are a special breed - to be able to make people look and feel good. Where else but in a salon do people come bearing gifts at Christmas, birthdays and sometimes for no reason - just because we are loved and appreciated.

"For Today We'll Find A Way" *to greet each client with vitality, just like they were our first client.*

June 27

"Self trust is the essence of heroism."
-Ralph Waldo Emerson

Believe in yourself! We lose so many good young stylists because they don't have the patience to go the distance to build their clientele.

Hairdressing is like any other business, we must set our goals, visualize them and never lose sight of where we want to be.

We must trust in ourselves and know anything we need to learn is out there - through classes we can attend. We must stay in tune to be the best professional we can be.

"For Today We'll Find A Way" *to trust in ourselves to make the right choices.*

June 28

"What wisdom can you find that is greater than kindness."   -Jean Jacques Ronsseau

I was working at the Midwest Show and a young girl came up to my booth and said, "Colleen, I take my state board in June and I have you to thank!" I looked at this young girl, all of 18, and I couldn't place her. She said, "Remember all the times I came to visit you in the salon and you said Amy, you can do it. You encouraged me to go to beauty school." She was in 6th grade at the time. She then gave me a hug and thanked me for the encouragement.

It's nice to know that time with the young people is appreciated.

"For Today We'll Find A Way" *to be kind and show people we care.*

June 29

"If we all pulled in one direction, the world would keel over."   *-Yiddish Proverb*

There is a reason why we are all different and special. We all have much to contribute in the short time we are here.

Let's all pull together and find what world peace is all about. We have to find peace within ourselves first. The 90's have been proclaimed the Decade of the Hairdresser by, Arnie Miller. He is a hairdresser and knows how to create excitement in our profession. His enthusiasm is contagious, and his honest way of showing us his love, can mean as much to you as it does to me.

"For Today We'll Find A Way" *to get out there and show the world why we're here!*

June 30

"We know what a person thinks not when he tells us what he thinks, but by his actions."
                                    -Isaac Bashevis Singer

Don't we all know people that say one thing and do another?

They might say, "I want to be the best stylist I can be," and yet, never go to educational programs without complaining.

How about having a salon meeting to suggest ways to bring in business? The same stylists that want to make a lot of money complain that they aren't going to give their services away. Now, they would rather have 100% of nothing than a smaller percentage of something.

Use team work and networking ideas to better all of us, so that we can all succeed!

"For Today We'll Find A Way" *to be open and have a good attitude and remember we all want success.*

July 1

"Love conquers all."   *-Unknown*

Do you believe every position you've ever had was your own choice? Or, do you believe that you were guided there to learn a valuable lesson?

We have a high school and beauty school senior working as an assistant, when she was fourteen, she was left by her mother, an alcoholic, to fend for herself. We all love this girl and feel she came to our salon because of a power greater than all of us. She's been living with local families that opened their hearts and homes to help her.

What would ever make a parent abandon a child? In this case, the disease of alcoholism.

"For Today We'll Find A Way" *so we can reach out to someone that needs our love and support and be thankful for the love that comes to us.*

July 2

"Nothing can bring you peace but yourself."
-Ralph Waldo Emerson

In my early days of hairdressing, I was too anxious to please. My clients would tell me their problems and I would worry until their next visit. I didn't know how to let go. In those early years, I had ulcers. I was nervous and took everything to heart. As my years in the business progressed, I realized how important it was for my clients to confide in me. They share things that they couldn't tell anyone else. But, I've learned that it doesn't become my problem.

Young stylists of today can take the Positive People skills and avoid the frustration.

"For Today We'll Find A Way" *to be thankful for the clients we have today. Let's use our skills to make their day better.*

July 3

"The only gift is a portion of thyself."
-Ralph Waldo Emerson

Dennis Millard is a great educator. He gives beyond the call of duty. He also teaches us how to be salon owners, not just hairdressers trying to run a business.

My first encounter with Dennis, was during his Salons Management 101. I had just gone through losing my whole staff, and as he talked, the tears started to roll down my cheeks. Thank God I was in the front row. Dennis saw the tears and called a break. He asked me what was wrong and I told him. He said the only way is up. He said absorb what you can and I'll stay after class and help you. He sat with me for hours and helped me design a plan to get my business back in the black.

"For Today We'll Find A Way" *to give a portion of ourselves and it will come back ten fold.*

July 4

"Do you know why it's so hard to keep a family together? Because God gives us the ingredients but he doesn't give us the recipe."   -Unknown

This is a time when so many families are having troubled times.

Alcohol and drug abuse have hit most families in one way or another. I feel it's common place that all members of a family are so busy making their own way. Everyone is wondering where they fit in.

Spiritual focus is where good roots begin. A family life is so special and yet it seems more and more, that it's hard to have success in families.

Priority is where we have to begin. It takes a lot of effort to keep a family together.

"For Today We'll Find A Way" *to be thankful for opportunities to make a difference with our own family.*

July 5

"We are rarely proud when we are alone."
-Voltaire

Have you ever noticed that our sense of pride comes when someone else recognizes us?

When we are alone, we tend to find all the things that are wrong with us. We all long to be perfect, to look perfect. Who could be more critical than we are with ourselves? Would you want to be anyone else but you? I think not, for we are all unique and special! As salon professionals we can make all our clients feel good about themselves. Everyone needs to hear they have pretty eyes, a nice smile, great hair. Sincere complements are never forgotten.

"For Today We'll Find A Way" *to see our own beauty.*

July 6

"We are always getting ready to live, but never living."   -Ralph Waldo Emerson

Haven't we all dreamed of greater things? As salon professionals maybe it's competition in hair design.

Imagine a silver or gold cup for a new design that you have created.

Is your dream being a salon manager, guiding other stylists to being better professionals?

How about owning your own salon? We all feel things would be run differently if we owned the salon. Well, we all have the same opportunities, depending on our own priorities.

"For Today We'll Find A Way" *to list all our dreams and set our goals.*

July 7

"The most beautiful experience we can have is the mysterious."   *-Albert Einstein*

I was working as a stylist in the Hair Em Salon inside the Aladdin Hotel in Las Vegas. There was an A.A. Convention in the hotel.

As I started to do this woman's hair, she said that she was from Florida. I said, "Oh, my father lives in Florida!" To make a long story short, she knew my dad and was in his A.A. group. Then she asked if she could mention she had met me and I said, "Sure!" Two days later, when I came home from work, my son Jamie said, "MOM! Someone's on the phone who says he's my grandfather!" Through this woman, I was able to make amends with my father and find some inner peace in the process.

"For Today We'll Find A Way" *to understand our Higher Power may work in mysterious ways.*

July 8

"True ambition is not what we thought it was. True ambition is the profound desire to live usefully and walk humbly under the grace of God."   -Bill W.

My ambition as a young girl was to be the best owner-hairdresser I could be. My goals were etched in my brain.

Now my deepest ambition is to take the time to make a difference in the lives I touch. My true focus is to try to understand other peoples' feelings and why fate has brought us together. If I practice this focus in all my affairs, I will succeed in being the best salon professional I can be.

"For Today We'll Find A Way" *to tune in to our surroundings and be happy with the journey we have before us.*

July 9

"First keep the peace within yourself, then you can also bring peace to others."   -Thomas A. Kempis

Ah! Inner peace, something everyone wants and only a few can grasp.

Working in the salon for a quarter of a century, I've seen friction and frustration in trying to work with so many personalities. It's totally amazing how much we each have to offer.

Team spirit and sharing is the key to clients having a good experience in our salons.

As we work side by side, let's try and keep our own personal focus and as we love unconditionally, we will find our own peace.

"For Today We'll Find A Way" *to keep focus to find our own peace and then hope it's contagious.*

July 10

"Exuberance is beauty."   *-William Blake*

When you see exuberance in someone, do you see a natural beauty in them? Have you ever known someone that was beautiful to you, but not particularly attractive?

Have you ever felt the exuberance of a big beauty show? It's a feeling that is hard for me to describe. We check into the hotel and my excitement begins to mount. I can never sleep before a big show.

I'm so lucky to be a part of the total picture in our beauty industry. The great thing is, I see that look on everyone's face at the shows. We are in this to go the distance and make a difference.

"For Today We'll Find A Way" *to remember our excitement after a show. How can we use something we have learned?*

July 11

"Courage is doing what your afraid to do. There can be no courage unless you are scared."
-Eddie Kickenbacker

Courage was definitely in order on that cold crisp January day in New York City, when my friend Frances and I were on the Phil Donahue Show.

When Marlaine Selip, the producer called me and asked if I was seeing anyone I told her no. She said, "we are doing a show on single women who haven't been involved for over a year." We talked about what I'd look for in a relationship and what kind of boundaries I had. We also talked about the concern of disease and as responsible adults what that meant.

Frances and I were on the show and the title under our name was "currently celibate." We laughed so hard - it sure sounded different than uninvolved!

"For Today We'll Find A Way" *to have the courage to laugh at ourselves.*

July 12

"The difficulty in life is the choice."   *-Unknown*

　I spent a few hours with some old friends, and it felt so good to look at the positive changes in their lives.

　The Murphy brothers will always be a part of my independence. Some years ago they lent me money and showed me their faith and trust. They will always have a special place in my heart. I guess the song, "I've Got A New Attitude" reminds me of the closeness and changes we've all been through.

"For Today We'll Find A Way" *to remember we have the power to make all our own choices. Let's start today making the best choice we can to better ourselves.*

July 13

"Be not afraid of life. Believe that life is worth living and your belief will help create the fact. Be not afraid to live."   *-William James*

My first experience of being on the Phil Donahue Show, the subject was "Armchair Psychology." I shared the stage with a bartender, cab driver and a stewardess. It was a fun experience and I know I projected the caring of most hairdressers. I told a few funny stories about life in the salon.

Phil asked me what makes our clients confide in us? My response was, "Our clients look to us not only to look good, but for the nurturing and caring that makes them feel good."

"For Today We'll Find A Way" *to live each and every day to the fullest.*

July 14

"One MAN with courage is a majority."
-Andrew Jackson

At first I was reluctant to include a motivational statement that referred only to a man. In our world of professionals, I have never felt any kind of discrimination because I'm a female.

I guess I learned about a woman's place from my mother - a woman's place is everywhere.

We all go through times, man or woman, that we feel unsure, but once we make a commitment to ourselves, we are halfway there.

We are fortunate in our field that we are a team and we can achieve anything we have the courage to put our minds to.

"For Today We'll Find A Way" *to have the courage to progress on our journey. What will your most courageous act be? A color, a perm or a hug?*

July 15

"Being wise is to give because it makes you feel good. In short, the wise person is the ordinary person doing extraordinary things." -Arnie Miller

We all have certain character defects because no one is perfect. Time reveals all of these in one way or another. I spent most of my life trying to please my mother, my children and my husband. I spent a lot of frustrated years until I realized I had to please myself or I would never have inner peace. I finally started standing up for what I wanted and everyone has more respect for me - including me!

When we are upset because we can't afford new shoes, think of the person without feet. If we all take a few moments to be kind to others we may find peace in this world of ours yet!

"For Today We'll Find A Way" *to make our ordinary tasks turn out extraordinary.*

July 16

"Every man has a right to be valued by his best moment."   -Ralph Waldo Emerson

I remember the first time I saw the Altieri Brothers work on stage. They have such energy and excitement. Watching Tony and Ricco do power cutting, which they made so big in our midwest area, was thrilling. The way their shears slide through the hair with the blades hardly moving. I went to the model room and watched every move and asked questions. What showmen! The enthusiasm that Heinz, Tony and Ricco brought to that stage is something I'll never forget.

I tried the power cut on my cousin Marilyn without razor edge shears. She complained, but I said, "Sit still, you'll look great."

The next morning I was back at the show and Ricco helped me choose my new power shears.

"For Today We'll Find A Way" *to appreciate all the times friends like Heinz, Tony, and Ricco show us the way.*

July 17

"Successful people are made up of two groups. F&G negative are 70% driven by fear and greed. F&G positive are 30% driven by faith and gratitude."
                                        -Dan O'Brien

Dan is my cousin and has helped me with my salon. His common sense approach has helped him be very successful.

F&G negative people are motivated, hard working, wheeler dealers that reach all their goals, but have no inner peace when they get there.

F&G positive people are driven by faith and gratitude. They help others achieve their goals, make money in the process, have fun and also have inner peace.

Which successful group will you be in when all is said and done?

"For Today We'll Find A Way" *to strive to be faith and gratitude oriented in everything we do. Let's help one another to be successful.*

July 18

"There is no security on this earth - there is only opportunity."   *-Douglas McArthur*

What is security? The dictionary describes it as 1) safety, 2) protection, 3) pledge given on a loan, 4) certificate of stock.

All of my life, I strived for security. Giving my children the best and letting them know how much I love them. I realize now what I bought my children wasn't all that important, because toys and clothes are soon forgotten. The love we show for our children will give them the most important treasure, their self esteem. I wish I knew then, what I know now, that positive reinforcement can make the difference in anyone's life.

"For Today We'll Find A Way" *to keep our young people safe and protect them from negative self esteem.*

July 19

"Sometime they'll give a war and nobody will come."
-Carl Sandburg

Imagine the greatness of that quote. World peace I hope will be something seen in our lifetime. The 90's are already showing a lot of promise.

Do you remember when it was unheard of for one salon to be friends with another salon in the same area? Well things are changing and successful salon professionals realize by sharing our knowledge with each other, we can all get stronger and better. I can't think of a day better spent than with other professionals sharing ideas.

"For Today We'll Find A Way" *to make the first move in being friendly to another salon.*

July 20

"The scars you acquire by exercising courage will never make you feel inferior."   -D.A. Battista

I remember how devastated I felt going through my second divorce. Through much anguish and lots of heartache, I realized that the only way to succeed and find an inner peace was to leave Andy. He is still a dear friend and a good father. I can truly say I'm glad we shared ten years together but sometimes we grow in different directions and for everyone concerned, it's best to move on.

Let go of the old guilts and heaviness from the past and look to a brighter future.

"For Today We'll Find A Way" *to have the courage to stand up for what we believe in.*

July 21

"Tain't worthwhile to wear a day out before it comes."   *-Sara Orne Jewett*

We can all remember a day we waited for with such anticipation, that we drove ourselves crazy. Then the day arrived and it just wasn't what we thought it would be.

Spending our day enjoying each and every experience we have is a divine gift.

Our lives are gifted if we take the time to recognize each beautiful experience.

We have team work in our salon now. In the past we had some frustrating days because that's what we chose it to be. What we were really experiencing was a minor inconvenience as the great Dr. Lew Losoncy would tell us.

"For Today We'll Find A Way" *to be thankful for the Dr. Lew's in our lives.*

July 22

1) Develop a dream for your business.
2) Set up goals for your business.
3) Establish a plan for your business.
-Dennis Millard

Dennis is a true professional. While taking his class, I was overwhelmed with what I didn't know. He took me aside and helped me chart my course.

If you have ever wanted to chart your way to success, his class is a must. As a stylist, he can help you run your clientele like a business.

I think what makes Dennis so special is he has had the rough times too, but has grown from it and never forgotten how he started.

"For Today We'll Find A Way" *to have our dreams set with written goals that are affirmed each day - success is inevitable.*

July 23

"Do it now! I expect to pass through this world but once. Any good thing, therefore, that I can do or show to any fellow human being, let me do it now. Let me not defer nor neglect it, for I shall not pass this way again."   -Stephen Grellet

When we think about how important each day is, how can we waste a minute?

None of us can make it through this world alone so why not give it our best shot and leave this world a better place by being here.

Take a few moments this beautiful day to try and be kind to every person you encounter. If we can do it for one day - why not all days?

"For Today We'll Find A Way" *to do it now!*

July 24

"To be confident is to act in faith." -Bernard Bynion

My confidence comes from my faith in my spiritual focus. Each day when I awake, I take quiet time to collect my thoughts and read my affirmation books. It sets my mood for the day. I've had days where I got side tracked and missed doing my reading and my day was off - something wasn't right!

Did you know if you want to make a habit of something, if you do it twenty-one days in a row, you'll have made it a habit. Good habits are made one day at a time.

"For Today We'll Find A Way" *to use inner focus to have a confident day. Then, we can welcome change knowing we are focused.*

July 25

"The remedy of all blunders, the cure of blindness, the cure of crime, is love." -Ralph Waldo Emerson

Let me tell you about Nellie, a wonderful salon professional. I had the pleasure of working with her for about six years.

The day Nellie interviewed for a stylist position, she walked into a madhouse. Clients were waiting all over. I said, "I wish I could talk to you but I'm not even officially opened yet and business is pouring in!" Being a take charge person, she said, "Let me get my shears out of the car and I'll help you!" It was the beginning of a great friendship as well as a team to build the salon together.

Nellie is now in Florida, but we still miss her in the burbs of Chicago!

"For Today We'll Find A Way" *to lend a hand. It could help your career and create a friend for life.*

July 26

"Being wise is being a nice person, willing to work, with an inquisitive mind open to challenge and change." —Arnie Miller

Do we look at each day as an adventure or a chore? Life is mostly what we make of it.

I've been through some rough times in my life, as I have shared with all of you. Through it all, I knew if I treated others the way I wanted to be treated and searched for ways to make my own personal peace within myself, my challenges would be met and good changes were inevitable. When times were tough, I escaped into my work. It never failed me. How many people love what they do? I'm lucky, because I do.

"For Today We'll Find A Way" *to set our inquisitive minds for good changes.*

July 27

"Don't forget one thing hasn't changed - we're still in a business that allows us the opportunity to not only make somebody look better, but to also make them feel better."   -Arnie Miller

We have a wonderful client named Barb. She is a beautiful woman inside and out. She is such a caring person. She's tall, has a great figure with beautiful silver hair.

She takes her aunt shopping and to lunch every week on her day off. She also cares for her family in such a loving way. It makes me feel so good that she chooses to share her life with me. We have grown to be confidants. Do we really realize how important we are in each others lives?

"For Today We'll Find A Way" *to not only make our clients look good, but feel good too!*

July 28

"People have evolved through the ages - from the Stone Age, Industrial Revolution and the Space Age to what I now call the Age Of The Survival Of The Wisest."   *-Arnie Miller*

On our journey, it's so important to take time to remember the people that helped us get to where we are today.

So many people want recognition for everything and take credit for knowing all the answers. Do you think anyone can succeed without other people helping along the way?

There are so many wealthy, unhappy people in existence because the way they achieved success was by stepping on others to get what they wanted.

"For Today We'll Find A Way" to be happy for the kind, caring friend we all have in Arnie Miller. Happy Birthday Arnie!!

July 29

"WISE is using your combination of skills, talents, creativity, compassion. It's believing, dreaming and daring. It means you understand that you have to be a self-starter. That you're willing to give, not take."
-Arnie Miller

What a man who practices what he preaches! Arnie Miller is truly a leader in our industry. He is the kind of man that loves to see others succeed. He has many, many self starters in his life and always is making room for more.

Are you going to join Arnie's Army? Believe in yourself and know if we all share our experience with each other, we will have a winning team.

"For Today We'll Find A Way" *to give of ourselves. Let's all dream big, set our goals and be daring.*

July 30

"In order to be WISE, one needs to be kind, encouraging, aggressive and tolerant, while having the ability to use the abundance of information that is available."   -Arnie Miller

The decade of the hairdresser, proclaimed by the big guy, Arnie Miller himself, means we are finally coming into our own.

I think of how I started twenty seven years ago with all my hopes and dreams. It has been such a journey for me. I only hope that the young stylists out there can give themselves a chance to stay in this wonderful business. Set a goal of two years and commit to building up a clientele and get out there and do it.

"For Today We'll Find A Way" *to encourage and train our future young stylists for success.*

July 31

"One needs to have a mind open to changes and challenges, in addition to a willingness to work hard and think."   -Arnie Miller

    I would have never believed that I would have clients that would perm and color in the same day. I used to think they'll never spend that kind of money. They do, and most of all they like the convenience.

    Just because things worked one way doesn't mean we shouldn't invite change. We are in such a progressive business. We must be willing to go with the flow and be create changes to make our work easier and better. Work smart, not hard!

"For Today We'll Find A Way" *to keep open minds to grow as salon professionals.*

August 1

"What is right for you is what you must do. Just remember to treat your clients the way you personally want to be treated and you'll find success that will carry you to the year 2000."
-Arnie Miller

Sometimes it's good to go on a busman's holiday. Do you ever critique service people?

Let's imagine all of our clients are going to grade our performance today. Would they say it was a good experience, or would they say a great experience? Let's suppose they were going to publish the results in *Modern Salon*. Would we be proud of our work?

"For Today We'll Find A Way" *to take the few extra minutes to make our clients feel as SPECIAL as they really are.*

August 2

"When the student is ready, the teacher appears."
-Unknown

Readiness has everything to do with how much we learn. Opportunity always seems to knock on our door when we are ready for some answers.

There are many reasons why the institute programs are so near and dear to me. For me, I was ready to grow as a professional. How lucky we are to gain so much knowledge at such a small cost.

It amazes me how some people would rather complain that they have no business and things are slow in the salon, rather than realize they could succeed with an educational experience of a lifetime.

"For Today We'll Find A Way" *to make changes. So start today with education so we can earn a prosperous living.*

August 3

"When we <u>realize</u> a total concept of something, as <u>we are experiencing it</u>, we are for that moment perfect."
—Jacquelyn Small

Sitting in on a Dennis Millard class, working with an adding machine (bookwork has never been my forte), I was a bit confused on the concept. Cheryl one of my team members said, "Did you get it yet?" I said, "No, I'm confused." She helped me and in a matter of two minutes, she taught me Dennis' concept. It was like someone turned on the light for me. Yes, now I can keep good records with relative ease. Now that I understand how, I can keep better records!

Thanks Cheryl and Dennis for sharing your knowledge with me.

"For Today We'll Find A Way" *to reach out to help others feel perfect at least for a moment.*

August 4

"I found that I could find the energy, that I could find the determination to keep on going. I learned that your mind can amaze your body, if you just keep telling yourself, I can do it. I can do it. I can do it."
-Jon Erickson

Have you ever heard the expression, "When you need something done, ask a busy person"? Enthusiasm is something you can't give someone else but you can have an infectious effect on others. The only determination is in our own minds.

Have you often wondered why one stylist can have five perms and lots of color work while another stylist can sit and complain how bad business is?

"For Today We'll Find A Way" *to accept that our belief is the determining factor in our success. We can do it. We can do it. We can do it!*

August 5

"It is better to light a candle, than curse the darkness."   *-Chinese Proverb*

Doesn't everyone have a dark area in their lives? A place no one else knows about? I feel when we look to others expecting perfection, let's all remember, we can expect perfection when we are perfect ourselves.

Everything looks better when we shed a little light on it, so when things look their darkest, why not light a candle?

When we start to trust each other with our inner thoughts, the world will be much brighter for all of us.

"For Today We'll Find A Way" *to look to the brighter side of things and be happy for the light in our world.*

August 6

"Fortune and love befriend the bold."   *-Ovid*

I've always felt that being a leader was better for me. Each time in my life, when I tried to follow the crowd, my life literally went down the tubes. Usually, our instincts will warn us when something isn't right. But, self will, run amuck, can cause us a lot of undue pain.

Now that I have focus in my life, fortune and love are mine. Fortune being the chance each day to make a difference in the lives we touch. Love being the caring love of friends and family. For me, letting go and letting my God guide me was the answer.

"For Today We'll Find A Way" *to ask for spiritual guidance and our journey will be much easier.*

August 7

"Use your ears before your shears."
          -Dr. Lew Losoncy

My sister's friend, Jackie, comes into my salon. I've been doing her hair for a few years. Sometimes I have to remember that no matter how many years I've been doing hair, our clients know what they want.

I saw Jackie at my sister's house and commented on how nice her hair looked. She said, "This is how I want it cut, so the sides are short but tapers into the back." I said, "Okay.". Then she told me how sometimes I don't listen.

Jackie is an introvert, so it must have been very difficult for her to share her feelings with me. I'm glad she told me so I don't make that mistake again. Corrective criticism helps us grow into the person we want to be.

"For Today We'll Find A Way" *to remember, even though we've known someone for a long time, let's not take them for granted.*

August 8

"There is always free cheese in a mousetrap."
-American Proverb

Lots of times the easy way out isn't the best way.

Have you ever worked with a stylist that hustles all the business, greediness takes over and all they see is the dollar signs. Then, there's the stylist that takes the time and works as a true professional by suggesting a color, perm, or retail goods. In the long run, the true professional does better by building a secure following.

How many clients did the greedy stylist lose by hurrying through their service.

When the opportunity arises to grab something that isn't yours for the taking, remember, the first class action is doing the right thing.

"For Today We'll Find A Way" *to make today the first day of the rest of our lives to become the professional we want to be.*

August 9

"True freedom is to share, all the chains our brothers wear, and with heart and hand, to be earnest to make others free."
                           -James Russell Lowell

While I was going through my second divorce, I was having a hard time putting things into perspective. The trauma my children were going through and my own mixed emotions.

I decided to help people that were in rehabilitation after having nervous breakdowns. It was good for me to realize how lucky I was. I walked in and saw a girl I went all through school with. She was very intelligent and I assumed she was one of the counselors. I told her I was there to help people learn good hygiene, hair and skin care. My old friend told me she was a patient.

My heart ached for her and what she had been through. I was glad to give an old friend a hug.

"For Today We'll Find A Way" *to recognize that the more good we can do for others, the more it comes back to us.*

August 10

"Helping the people around us is when we grow the most."   *-Arnie Miller*

The team of people I work with at the hair shows are totally in tune with helping each other.

When setting up a big show, we start on Friday and by Sunday we have it all in place.

We set up the booths, arrange the displays, set-up bag deals, collate literature on new products. To be a part of it, is really something.

Sore feet are soon forgotten when the first design team gets up on the stage to show us the latest trends.

We all sing to the familiar theme songs we know and love.

"For Today We'll Find A Way" *to enjoy our shows that make us better prepared to help each other to succeed. Happy Birthday Sydell!!!*

August 11

"Freedom is the right to choose; the right to create for yourself alternatives of choice. Without the exercise of choice, a man is not a man but a member, an instrument, a thing."
            -Archibald MacLeish

We all think about freedom. As children we take direction from our parents. What about when we grow old? We will be there someday with any luck.

One morning, I was bringing some fruit to my friend Lonnie who lives in an old folks home. Lonnie was sitting in the lounge, very upset. She said that there was trouble with the air conditioning. Of course, this was one of the hottest days of the year (105 degrees). Lonnie and her roommate came home with me to spend the night. What about the other people that had no one to care? Sometimes it's hard to exercise freedom without help.

"For Today We'll Find A Way" *to bring life into perspective by choosing to bring joy into the lives of others.*

August 12

"In order to change someone, I must first change me."   *-Carole Lyden Smith*

Can we talk? I spent the first nineteen years of my son Jamie's life, trying to control him. What I realize now, is that my son has my spirit for life, and feared he would make the same mistakes I had.

When someone frustrates us, we must go within for the answers.

Jamie is very capable and is now twenty three years old. We have a wonderful relationship. He is learning his own focus, so he can guide his son, Zachary, to be all he can be.

We are all here to serve one another. There are no mistakes.

"For Today We'll Find A Way" *to take a personal inventory and go within for the answers. Happy Birthday, Jamie!*

August 13

"Much of your pain is self chosen. It is the bitter potion by which the physician within you heals your sick self."
                                        -Kahil Gibran

    My niece, Linda, fell in love with a young man named Robert. Our family discouraged her from seeing him. I can remember telling her what a rough life she was choosing for herself and for Robert.

    Robert and Linda have a son named Matthew. He is so full of love and has the happiest disposition. He is 3 years old. My niece is a very lucky girl because she looks through eyes that are not blinded by color. Robert is bi-racial. I feel fortunate that Robert is in our family.

    Try and understand the definition of prejudice; opinions formed without basis.

    Our family has learned to let go of prejudice for only we can break the chains of the past.

"For Today We'll Find A Way" *to heal any prejudices we have and join hands to make our world a better place.*

August 14

"A man's reach should exceed his grasp or what's a heaven for?"   *-Robert Browning*

How often have we reached our goals, and then realized half the fun is the struggle?

Each day that our salon grows by giving good service and suggesting multiple services, it makes me so happy, that I love this profession.

So many clients have had horrible experiences in a salon. I'm glad our team keeps growing one step at a time.

Do you greet your client within three to five seconds with a handshake and a smile, and thank them for coming in? Isn't it a good start?

We all have so many things to share with each other to better all our businesses.

"For Today We'll Find A Way" *to make our salons a pleasant experience for our clients.*

August 15

"In order to succeed, we must first believe we can."
-Michael Korda

When I met my client and friend, Velma, she had long hair in an updo in big curls, and it was bleached with a bluish cast. She was very set in her ways and is afraid of change, but also a take charge person. One day a client asked. "Is she nice to work for?" That's right, they thought she was the owner. Velma has gone through a lot of changes. She now has blond hair done in a short, chic style.

When Dr. Lew Losoncy says we transform destinies, I guess he's right - one moment at a time.

"For Today We'll Find A Way" *to look at our client list and transform some destinies.*

August 16

"In the moment that you carry this conviction...in that moment your dream will become a reality."
-Robert Collier

All my life I thought I'd like to write a book, and yet, in the back of my mind, I thought I can't do that. But yes I can, by sharing some rough times and happy times with all of you. The point I'd most like to make is, "We can do whatever we set our minds to!"

What can we all do to make our lives happier? I start each morning with a quiet time. I read several affirmation books that set my mood for the day. It's amazing what we can accomplish when our lives have focus.

"For Today We'll Find A Way" *to have the conviction to realize our dreams.*

August 17

"The future of our industry is the children, we must guide our future stylists to success."
                                    -Dennis Millard

    A good portion of my career has been helping young stylists to find their way. It's one of the most satisfying parts of my profession.
    If we want to continue to have good stylists to work with we must take the time to educate them.
    I don't think there's a better feeling than to see a look of confidence and creativity on a new member of our team.
    I'm thankful to be able to help create careers for such deserving young people. It sure beats complaining that there's a shortage of good hairdressers.

"For Today We'll Find A Way" *to take the time to help each other grow, and grow, and grow.*

August 18

"If you don't recommend products for clients' use at home, it's okay with me. But if you don't, then give me your moussette and your styling gel and style your clients' hair with water. Because if you need it, they need it."   *-Arnie Miller*

Aren't we lucky to have so many wonderful products to create any kind of style our minds can imagine?

An easy way to get your clients to use our products is to educate them. I just say, "If I could do your hair with water, do you think I would pay for all these products?" We must educate our clients! After I apply something, I set the bottle in their lap so they can smell the fragrance and read what it does for their hair. We must make recommendations and close with, "Would you like the eight ounce or sixteen ounce size?"

"For Today We'll Find A Way" *to recommend the products our clients need. Keep a record and on their next visit, ask how they liked it.*

August 19

"Be not afraid of life. Believe life is worth living and your belief will help create the fact."
-William James

Have you ever crossed paths with a person from your past who had really hurt you?

The girl from my past, was at a party at a mutual friend's house. I can remember how crushed I was when she pulled the rug out from under me. As I look back, I was the lucky one. The girl hasn't grown as a person. Fear and greed are a part of her every day life. In listening to her, she really didn't have a nice word for anyone, not even her own friends around her. In the few hours of listening to her, most of her conversation was negative.

I'm thankful to be a part of this great world.

"For Today We'll Find A Way" *to look at our journey with faith and gratitude, and let go of old hurts.*

August 20

"People don't want to be sold, they want to be a part of something."   *-Arnie Miller*

The 90's have brought team work to an all time high.

To achieve success in the salon we must all set our egos aside and help one another.

When one stylist gets backed up, doesn't it make you feel good to pitch in and give them a hand?

Our clients feel a part of our salon enthusiasm. Some of our clients like coming to the salon for company, as well as getting their hair done.

In our fast paced busy world, to extend warmth, caring and genuine concern for people, can be the difference in the success of our salons.

"For Today We'll Find A Way" to share our lives with everyone. Hugs always feel good.

August 21

"Hair fashion comes from the mood of society."
   -Dwight Miller

My stylist, Cari, and I attended a hair convention in Cleveland. It was our pleasure to see Dwight Miller work. To watch Dwight work, is to watch one of the masters of our time. His shears glide through the hair. It's no wonder he sets the trends. He really is way ahead of our time. If you've ever had the pleasure of watching him work, I know you'll understand my feeling of awe.

"For Today We'll Find A Way" *to learn the trends that will keep us at the top of our profession.*

August 22

"A recent survey pointed out that two-thirds of the public choose their hairstylist based on people skills (high touch). Only one-third said they picked their hairstylist for technical skills (high tech)."
-Arnie Miller

Although we follow the trends and learn new techniques and styles, through Salon Psychology education, we keep our clientele by understanding their lifestyle . We have learned why certain people react a certain way.

Change is so important for personal growth. If we don't ever suggest change, our clients will find a stylist that does. Clients that stay stuck in one time zone, really need our help even more. Understand and again, suggest subtle changes.

"For Today We'll Find A Way" *to touch our clients by letting them feel as special as they really are.*

August 23

"When we concentrate on what it is that we do best, we'll meet...and yes, even exceed the customers' expectations." -Arnie Miller

Our salon is a fun place to be. We feel our clients should not only have their hair done well, but also experience a mini vacation from their busy lives.

We serve coffee, ice tea, cookies, coffee cake and candy. Our clients are greeted and welcomed the minute they come in.

We also use a softsell approach by suggestion. We never assume someone only wants a haircut. We like to offer different options. Even a simple colorizing with a hint of color can offer gloss and shine to a client's hair. We feel it's better than a pick me up bouquet, and certainly makes someone feel better.

"For Today We'll Find A Way" *to suggest alternative changes to our clients and follow through each visit.*

August 22

"A recent survey pointed out that two-thirds of the public choose their hairstylist based on people skills (high touch). Only one-third said they picked their hairstylist for technical skills (high tech)."
-Arnie Miller

Although we follow the trends and learn new techniques and styles, through Salon Psychology education, we keep our clientele by understanding their lifestyle . We have learned why certain people react a certain way.

Change is so important for personal growth. If we don't ever suggest change, our clients will find a stylist that does. Clients that stay stuck in one time zone, really need our help even more. Understand and again, suggest subtle changes.

"For Today We'll Find A Way" *to touch our clients by letting them feel as special as they really are.*

August 23

"When we concentrate on what it is that we do best, we'll meet...and yes, even exceed the customers' expectations." *-Arnie Miller*

Our salon is a fun place to be. We feel our clients should not only have their hair done well, but also experience a mini vacation from their busy lives.

We serve coffee, ice tea, cookies, coffee cake and candy. Our clients are greeted and welcomed the minute they come in.

We also use a softsell approach by suggestion. We never assume someone only wants a haircut. We like to offer different options. Even a simple colorizing with a hint of color can offer gloss and shine to a client's hair. We feel it's better than a pick me up bouquet, and certainly makes someone feel better.

"For Today We'll Find A Way" *to suggest alternative changes to our clients and follow through each visit.*

August 24

"Visualization or mental imagining, is a powerful skill that can be practiced regularly to improve your on-the job performance."   -Dr. Fred Elias

Do we look at ourselves as successful professionals?

In the past, I've had many problems. My life sure was out of sync. I was anxious, lived with a knot in my stomach, and had a fairly short fuse. My self esteem was very low. So, what people saw, wasn't the way I really felt.

Mental imagining or visualization has been a big part of my own personal recovery.

Each morning I spend a few quiet moments reading my daily affirmation books and then I close my eyes and meditate on the positive focus in my life. Thoughts come and go, and you'll learn to feel the serenity that I feel each day.

"For Today We'll Find A Way" *to have quiet time to focus our life each day and peace will be ours.*

August 25

"You (the hairdresser of the 90's), will be a professional who succeeds through mastery of technical and people skills."   -Arnie Miller

I can't think of a better time to be a professional hairdresser. We are now recognized as true professionals in the community.

A client, that I had for a long time had a growth on her forehead. I suggested she have it looked at, and she said she would. Well, time passed and I could see the growth changing. So I would encourage her each week to have it checked. She finally went to a plastic surgeon and he said, "It's a good thing your hairdresser is a good professional." She then asked if she could still have her hair done and he said, "Your hairdresser will know how to treat it."

"For Today We'll Find A Way" to take the time to really look at our clients in case they need medical attention.

August 26

"Outside show is a poor substitute for inner worth."
-Aesop

I have a dear friend and client named Sean. He's a nice young man about my son Jamie's age. He's so patient when he comes in for a haircut. It seems no matter when I book him the salon is always jammed.

I feel very close to Sean. I told him if he ever wants to use the pool at my condo he's always welcome. Sean came by when it was approximately 100 degrees. Later, I brought him out a sandwich and we sat down with a couple of my elderly neighbors. We were all joking about our freckles connecting so we'd look tan. Sean said, "It doesn't matter how we look on the outside as long as we're beautiful on the inside."

Friends can be any age, if we let them into our world.

"For Today We'll Find A Way" *to look inside and see someone's beauty.*

August 27

"The barrier between success is not something which exists in the real world; it is composed purely and simply of doubts about ability."
                              -Marke Caine

Have you ever noticed the difference in successful salon professionals? They have three things in my estimation. 1) They are driven. 2) They have a need to succeed. 3) They are focused.

I see differences in my assistants that are still in beauty school. I suppose some people think it's a fight, but in essence we all have to choose to either succeed or sit back and complain. I like a find-a-way attitude where success is important.

"For Today We'll Find A Way" *to have the ability to be all that we want to be, and we will continue to work towards our goals.*

August 28

"Getting an idea should be like sitting on a pin; it should make you jump up and do something."
-E.L. Simpson

I met this lady when I was about eighteen. She did my income taxes. I shared with her my hopes and dreams. Gladys is a find-a-wayer. Whenever I needed money for something, she offered it.

When someone believes in you and puts their money where their mouth is, you know deep down in your soul, you'll do what it takes to show them their belief wasn't misplaced.

Gladys is a kind and hard working woman. She has been my mentor, banker, bookkeeper (even when I couldn't pay her) and most of all, my friend.

"For Today We'll Find A Way" *to thank all the Gladys' in our lives and to always believe in our ideas and dreams.*

August 29

"We don't need to build better hairdressers, we need to develop more successful human beings."
-Dennis Millard

Our salon is based on focus. I feel so lucky that a force greater than me sends me good people.

We have an assistant named Angie. She is a hard-working, beautiful young woman. When she came to us, she was very introverted, and her hair kind of covered her face. She has blossomed into a self-assured professional with a great knowledge of our industry. She is an asset to our profession. She now wears her hair back and joins into our salon family.

We love Angie, and her growth through love and caring is very real.

"For Today We'll Find A Way" *to look at each person on our team as a part of our salon family and then reach new heights together.*

August 30

"If you want to know how to win, ask a winner."
-Dr. Lew Losoncy

If one stylist in the salon does a lot of color and perm work, wouldn't it make sense to ask them how they do it.

There are so many subtle color services with prisms or semi-permanent moderation or even so-colorizing. It's a lot easier to give a client a hint of color with a beautiful healthy shine, than trying to stand like a robot cutting all day.

You can also tell people nothing is more mood lifting and inexpensive than a hint of color. Your client may not have the money to go on vacation, but to perk up our looks with a perm or color costs much less and can really make you feel better.

"For Today We'll Find A Way" *to ask a winner how to increase our color and perm business.*

August 31

"All territories are the same, some just not developed. Outwork the competition."
-George Temple

I was lucky enough to be in the audience when George Tempo talked at our tenth anniversary soiree.

George talked about the importance of outworking the competition. We have to understand that people are influenced. If we use a soft-sell approach and suggest different services and retail products to our clients, they will buy. It is a proven fact, that the more you sell a client, the more they believe in you as a professional.

So let's dig in and work hard to increase our perm, color and retail business. It's time we all worked smart, not hard.

"For Today We'll Find A Way" *to suggest new services to all our clients today.*

September 1

"Money doesn't give you the pride of doing good for others. The dollars will come if we create the dream."   *-Dennis Millard*

If we base our lives on the faith and gratitude we have in each other, wouldn't our lives have more meaning?

I try to give back what I have been so lucky to receive. If we give of ourselves, all of our wants will be fulfilled. The only way I know how to have serenity and happiness, is to help others to achieve their dreams.

I feel so lucky to have found my own recovery, that I hope any of my fellow professionals that live with problems of addictions, dysfunction and turmoil, know there's a light at the end of the tunnel.

"For Today We'll Find A Way" *to start today helping people achieve their dreams.*

September 2

"I will see it when I believe it."   -*Carole Lyden Smith*

My little grandson Zachary was born on this day and weighed in at 1 pound, 15 ounces. Can you imagine how frightened we all were?

Little Zak had a rough start, but everyone we knew was focused on him making it. Everyone asked their higher power for help. I believe it worked out, because I saw it with my own eyes. At three weeks, he made it through surgery for intestinal blockage. The best one yet, was when he was eight weeks old, his respirator was down to 20% and he literally pulled the tube out of his throat and started breathing on his own. The doctor said, "He knows more than we do." Now I ask you, Why did one little Zak make it when so many don't? Great care for sure, but also greater faith!

"For Today We'll Find A Way" *to visualize. The faster we see it, and the more we can believe. He made it, he's a year old now. Happy Birthday, Zak!*

September 3

"Is it illusion or magic?"   *-Arnie Miller*

Our salon team works together like magic. We reach out to each other and every client feels they have our whole team support when making a decision for a new color or cut.

When a group of people are brought together to work side by side, and we each have so much to give one another, I believe this is an act of God.

Why does someone walk into our salon and not the one down the block? I feel so lucky to share my days with a staff that believes in me as much as I believe in them.

"For Today We'll Find A Way" *to be magicians in our salons. Thanks team, for your love and support!*

September 4

"Having A Winning Attitude! One, ability to change. Two, people that have the magic feel, the power to change internally. Three, successful people are driven by their own internal state."
-Dr. Lew Losoncy

One of my clients had a dream. As a young executive, he was invited to play golf at a very prestigious country club in the midwest. He came home and told his wife, "If there's one thing I hope I can afford in this lifetime, it would be to belong to that club. That's my heart's desire."

He is a man that has a dream, sets his goal and has a plan to make it happen. He and his wife have been members of that club for years.

Words shared by a client and the stylist, can change the course of our lives. I am thankful for all the clients that have shared their recipe for success.

"For Today We'll Find A Way" *to try a new recipe. It can taste so good to try something a new way and feel driven internally.*

September 5

"All the significant battles are waged within the self."
-Sheldon Kopp

I met a wonderful hairdresser at the Indiana Beauty Show. She's been a hairdresser for 62 years. She was 80 years old and still interested in seeing the latest in hair fashion. I don't remember her name, but I'll never forget how she shared her career with me. When she started out, they had to make their own shampoo by melting down bar soap. She was so enthusiastic about all the changes she's seen. She also said she's retired, but still does a few friends.

I guess with all the wonderful products, tools and education we have today, we are very lucky.

"For Today We'll Find A Way" to be the best if we so choose. What is your choice today?

September 6

"I like the dreams of the future better than the history of the past."   *-Thomas Jefferson*

Each day, as I reaffirm my goals and dreams, I also reflect and understand my past brought me to where I am today.

Guilt is a terrible thing to dwell on so I have learned to let go of the past and look to the dreams of the future.

You see, no matter what kind of a career you've had so far, you can start today fresh, and write down your goals so you can go forward.

If we have personal growth, we have everything. As I look back at where I was five years ago and where I am now, I am thankful for a new life.

"For Today We'll Find A Way" *to dream big, set our goals, dig in our heels, and go for it!*

September 7

"In the face of uncertainty, there is nothing wrong with hope."   *-Bernie Siegal, M.D.*

Have you read, *Love, Medicine, and Miracles?* What a wonderful book. There is always hope, and life will always be what we make it.

I have a client named Ester who went through surgery and chemotherapy, and not for one second did she give up. She lost most of her hair and had to quit getting perms and color, but her spirit was never broken. As soon as she could, she was back to work and restoring a townhouse at the same time.

Don't you wonder why some people come through strong, and others give up at the time of diagnosis?

"For Today We'll Find A Way" *to have a hopeful outcome no matter what we face.*

September 8

"Luck is a matter of preparation meeting opportunity."   -Oprah Winfrey

Have you ever heard the phrase, the harder I work the luckier I get?

When I go to the salon each day, every salon I pass is closed. I get an early start to prepare for my day. I feel if you run in at the last minute you'll feel disorganized all day.

I look over my client list to see who's going to need what. I also make notes on client cards to remember what I suggested so I can reaffirm. I also make notations on how many children, married, etc. It really makes a client feel good when you say "How's little Danny?"

"For Today We'll Find A Way" to prepare so we are ready for every opportunity we are given today.

September 9

"I don't think of all the misery, but of the beauty that still remains."   *-Anne Frank*

When I look back at some of the craziness in my past, I really am thankful for finding Adult Children Anonymous and the serenity that comes from working a twelve step program. Turning my life over to a power greater than myself, really does make a difference.

I went through most of my life feeling abandoned and really being numb to feelings at all.

I don't have any bad days, weeks or years anymore, and peace, serenity and unconditional love are the order of every day.

"For Today We'll Find A Way" *to look at the beauty around us, and be happy to live in a world where we can change anything, once we make up our own minds.*

September 10

"The more you give, the more you get."
-Arnie Miller

It's been said there are givers and takers. The longer I live, the more I see the only way to find peace and serenity is to give to others.

To give of oneself is the greatest gift of all. When we show support by listening and being there emotionally, it can be as good for us as it is for them. It doesn't mean giving solutions or answers. It just means we are giving comfort to help them through the rough times.

Arnie has given me so much. Being a part of Arnie's Army not only has given me the knowledge to be a better business woman, but to also be a better person.

"For Today We'll Find A Way" *to give of ourselves. The more we give, the more we get.*

September 11

"The only limit to our realization of tomorrow will be our doubt of today."   -Franklin D. Roosevelt

We all have the power to create change. We have to believe we will succeed.

If we live with truth, harmony and love, we will be guided to new heights.

The most important thing is never doubt our ability to grow.

Each time we feel we've made a mistake, haven't we learned something new?

Let's think of every day as a precious gift we've been given. What we choose to do, with each precious moment, is our own decision.

"For Today We'll Find A Way" *to not limit the visions of our future, by the narrow experiences of our past.*

September 12

"We can do only what we think we can do. We can be only what we think we can be. We can have only what we think we can have. What we do, what we are, what we have, all depends upon what we think."
-Robert Collier

Do we think we can be the best salon professional? My belief is, if I don't know it, I can learn it!

I remember in my early days when I would wear sweats or jeans to work. I'd think, "Oh, I'm not too busy. It doesn't matter." I'm here to tell you, one's image is very important. It's a proven fact when you dress as a professional, people will listen to what you say and value it.

"For Today We'll Find A Way" to dress for the salon, with the image we want to project.

September 13

"Love is above all, the gift of oneself."
-Jean Anouith

Love comes in all forms. The love my mom showed all of my six brothers and sisters and myself. My mom was mother and father to the seven of us. She really struggled to give us a good start. We were raised in a small town outside of Chicago.

My mom would say, "Babe, sing me a song" and I would. She made me think I could be a great singer, until I joined the chorus at school. So what can I say, my mom made each one of us feel special!

The fact that we were raised without a father left us all with a few scars and the love my family has given me makes me realize what my "dad" missed. I'm glad I made amends with him before he died, so I could let go of the pain.

"For Today We'll Find A Way" *to be thankful for the love and guidance that has brought us to where we are. Happy Birthday Mom!*

September 14

"If you will please people, you must please them in their own way; and as you cannot make them what they should be, you must take them as they are."
-Lord Chesterfield

We have all had clients that we wish would change their image. Dr. Lew Losoncy made me realize that people that stay the same are trapped in their own time zone. If they're still wearing their prom hairdo, it's because that's when they felt the prettiest.

Isn't it our job to make people look and feel good? If they're happy with their look and they feel good about themselves when they leave your chair, aren't we successful? When our client begins to trust, changes will occur. With clients like this a small change is a sign of trust.

"For Today We'll Find A Way" *to be successful if we make our clients feel and look good in their own way.*

September 15

"We must take responsibility for ourselves."
-Arnie Miller

My sister, Mary, invited me to her Lupus Support Group. Each person (with lupus) brought a family member. The goal was for the family member to have a better understanding of this baffling disease.

Much to my amazement, my sister led the discussion by telling about her fight with systemic lupus. Not only do I have better insight, I feel closer to my sister for sharing this evening with me. I learned that with lupus, you can appear well and be very sick at the same time.

It also dawned on me that my brothers and sisters and I share a gift for public speaking, and we all keep our sense of humor no matter what the situation.

"For Today We'll Find A Way" *to take ourselves less seriously and find a good sense of support when we need it.*

September 16

"Few people can fail to generate a self-healing process when they become genuinely involved in healing others."   -Theodore Isaac Rubin

Take it from a recovering co-dependent, we can't *fix* anyone but ourselves.

Don't we all know someone that's trying to fix us or control us in one way or another? The mark of co-dependency.

In the past, I tried to control and fix everyone and brought myself a lot of grief.

In the process of healing myself, I've come to believe in a power greater than myself, who could restore my sanity. I have learned to love unconditionally in the process.

"For Today We'll Find A Way" *to use our spiritual focus to bring about self healing, peace and serenity.*

September 17

"You have a remarkable ability which you never acknowledged before. It is to look at a situation and know whether you can do it, and I mean, really know the answer."   -Carl Frederick

Belief is a wonderful thing. Isn't it great to look at a head of hair, and know in your heart that you can do what your client wants?

In the past, if a client asked for something and I didn't know how to do it, I would use the "fake it till you make it" approach. Now all I have to do is pick up the phone and call my friends in the industry for some answers. I would rather tell a client, "Give me a week and I'll learn how to do it."

"For Today We'll Find A Way" *to have the belief that we can learn anything we set our minds to.*

September 18

"Live and let live."   *-Twelve Step Program Slogan*

We all have a big enough job taking care of ourselves.

When we judge others, aren't we taking time that could be well spent improving ourselves?

This world would really have problems if we all were the same.

Until we walk in someone else's shoes, it's impossible to understand what really has brought them to where they are.

To love unconditionally, is the greatest gift my higher power has ever given me.

I work on finding my own balance every day. When I care for someone, I know now, to caretake doesn't give them the chance for personal growth.

"For Today We'll Find A Way" to live and let live.

September 19

"People go to a salon to look and feel good."
-Arnie Miller

A client called the other day to ask if we were running any perm specials. I told her, "Yes, we're introducing a new perm," and told her where she could find our offer. She said, "I'll call you back for an appointment."

Connie called back and came in for her perm. She said the two reasons she came in were: because she called five other salons, and we were the friendliest, and because she likes the products we use.

Connie also told me when she was about to leave, that her experience in our salon was so great, she will be back and will send in her family and friends.

"For Today We'll Find A Way" *to remember why our clients come to us...to look and feel good.*

September 20

"When I repress my emotions, my stomach keeps score."   *-John Powell*

I lived most of my life by burying my feelings. If anyone asked how I was, fine was the answer. I lived with knots in my stomach all my life, never realizing that everyone doesn't live that way.

Through my Adult Children Anonymous program, I have learned to let go of the old hurts and anger. I have learned to live in the present and recognize my emotions. As a child, I didn't know how to cry. Living one day at a time is so much easier than overwhelming myself with the rest of my life.

I no longer stuff bad feelings. I have learned to live and enjoy my emotions.

"For Today We'll Find A Way" *to express one emotion today that takes some risk. We will learn to trust.*

September 21

"Love the moment and the energy of that moment will spread beyond all boundaries."   -Corita Kent

What gives our children the same idiosyncrasies we have?

I was sitting in my room writing this book, and I looked at my daughter, Kelly, lying on my bed reading the phone book, and I had to laugh. I said, "You and your dad, are the only two people I've ever known that would sit and read the phone book.

The way my son Jamie crosses his legs and cocks his head to one side when he's talking to someone, is like watching his father twenty years ago.

Life is such a wondrous thing, let's never waste it.

"For Today We'll Find A Way" to love each moment to the fullest and look at the beauty in all of life's little wonders.

September 22

"Changes (in life) are not only possible and predictable, but to deny them is to be accomplice to one's own unnecessary vegetation."   -Gail Sheehy

I have a friend named Bill. He is rigid in his way of life. Each day he sleeps a certain amount of hours, eats at certain times, leaves for work at exactly the same time each day. If anything upsets his apple cart, it really throws him. If each moment is predictable, we shut out all the little miracles life is all about.

To feel one's emotions and experience each moment to it's fullest, is what I feel contentment is all about. I'm thankful I've turned my life over, and my higher power guides me each moment.

"For Today We'll Find A Way" to welcome change and realize without it, we have no growth.

September 23

"Life is a succession of moments. To live each one is to succeed."   -Corita Kent

I was on the highway, on my way to an industry extravaganza. I was running late for model call and the red light in my car went on. As I pulled into the service station, my car was steaming and died. I went in to get some help, and within two minutes, I heard a loud boom and my car blew up. I ran out and said to a man standing outside, "I am so lucky!" He said (with a hoosier accent), "We've had cars blow up before, and not a one thought they were lucky." I said, "I am alive, and I can always buy a new car." He then said, "I guess that's what you'd call one of them positive attitudes, right?"

"For Today We'll Find A Way" *to understand that possessions can be replaced, moments can't. Live each one to the fullest.*

September 24

"The first and most important step toward success is the feeling that we can succeed."
                              -Nelson Boswell

One of the bright spots in my career, was checking out the model rooms at shows. After paying for a ticket, I would invariably be rinsing perms, helping clean up and whatever else was needed. People would say, "Why do you work for free?" My answer was, "Look what I've learned for free."

One day after the Midwest Show, Dorothy Lorenson and Frances Shunick took me aside and asked me to join their staff. I made the commitment and now I work behind the scenes and learn for free, plus collect a paycheck for doing what I love to do.

When someone says they can't afford the shows, I always mention my week-end gigs.

"For Today We'll Find A Way" to succeed in finding our own balance.

September 25

"The strongest single factor in prosperity consciousness is self esteem; believing you can do it, believing you deserve it, believing you will get it."
-Jerry Gillies

Working with our team has shown me there are no limits. Find a way, is the order of the day.

How many encouraging people have influenced your life? Think about it. Who gave you the feeling deep down in your heart, that you could achieve? We all deserve to be all that we can be.

We have a team that cares. Dr. Lew made me realize I have the ability to help others realize their potential. If we feel our calling, we can see goodness in everyone.

"For Today We'll Find A Way" *to believe we can do it, we deserve it, and we will get it.*

September 26

"Loneliness and the feeling of being unwanted is the most terrible poverty."   -Mother Teresa

When I was younger, I hated to be alone. When we isolate, we can feel alone in a room full of people.

In my search to find a better way, I've gone through many, many changes. They were all part of my own story. But, as I reflect, I really wouldn't change anything. It's what has brought me to where I am. To be able to love my fellow man unconditionally, regardless of their beliefs.

Wouldn't life be boring if we were all the same?

If I could give everyone I encounter one positive thought, it would be to love one another.

"For Today We'll Find A Way" *to look at what's right with people and we will find our own peace.*

September 27

"We don't make mistakes. We just have learnings."
-Anne Wilson Schaef

We all go through ups and downs. If we can treat each disappointment as a learning experience, we can go on our journey, and realize we can't appreciate the peaks without the valleys.

The hardest thing I have ever encountered, is to see someone I love, go through the same problems over and over. I believe in my heart, that until we learn what it is we need to learn, we will go through the same kinds of things over and over again.

"For Today We'll Find A Way" *to understand everyone is where they are, because that's where they need to be.*

September 28

"A man is literally what he thinks."   *-James Allen*

That goes for a woman too!

Do you fill your head with positive thoughts? I know that being positive is as natural to me as breathing. It's taken a lot of personal growth for me to rid myself of negative thoughts, but it can be done.

Encouragement is the cornerstone of helping others find a positive way of life. In the process of helping others achieve, I have found my personal peace.

As the great Dr. Lew always says, "If you want to be a winner, ask winners for advice."

"For Today We'll Find A Way" to surround ourselves with winners and encouragers.

September 29

"The mind is the limit. As long as the mind can envision the fact that you can do something, you can do it. As long as you really believe 100 percent."
-Arnold Schwarzenegger

Have you ever heard someone comment, 'I wish I could do that but I can't"? In their own way, they're right.

We must believe in our own minds that we can follow through and achieve, or we've lost already, because we don't believe in ourselves. As Norman Vincent Peale says, "What our minds believe, we can achieve."

If I have learned anything from my professional family, it is to have a find-a-way attitude. When we believe we can, we will succeed.

"For Today We'll Find A Way" *to make a list of our goals and focus on the most important one. We will affirm each morning the goal we have chosen, until it's a reality.*

September 30

"Plan your plan, study your lines, role play and get your timing down."   -Dennis Lubin

As in any service business, we must have goals. In order to reach our goals, whether in service or retail, we must have a plan.

Retailing was unheard of in the beauty industry when I started out 27 years ago. Now it's a big part of our income.

We can determine what products our clients are using by doing a consultation. How can we be professional without taking this step? We must educate our clients, and in the process of doing so, they will respect and look to us for the answers on how to look and feel good.

If we remind our clients that we can't do their hair without the right products, how can they? Suggestive selling is the answer.

"For Today We'll Find A Way" *to take the time today to educate each and every client we see.*

October 1

"I'd like to make a motion that we face reality."
-Bob Newhart

Many people go through life wishing and hoping that they'll achieve greatness, and their lives will be filled with good luck.

The reality of having one's dreams come true, is to have a plan. List our dreams, set our goals and have a plan of action.

My cousin, Dan, recommends using the kiss method - keep it simple, stupid.

If we are only doing ten percent (of our service) in retail, a realistic goal would be twenty percent.

We owe it to our clients to take care of their hair like a doctor takes care of their body.

"For Today We'll Find A Way" *to realize, the reality is, if we don't give our client good service, there's someone who will.*

October 2

"Give what you have. To someone it may be better than you think." -Henry Wadsworth Longfellow

When we grow old, do you think the quality of our lives will be gauged by how much money we've made? How we did at our chosen career? How big our house is?

I feel our lives will reflect exactly how we served others. Have we taken the time to be good to people? Have we given love unconditionally to the lives we've touched? Did we look for the good in others? Did we give from our hearts, not just what was expected?

Did we give our knowledge to the young people starting our in our profession? To share our experience not only helps them, it makes us feel good. We can also learn from them. The more we give the more we get.

"For Today We'll Find A Way" to give from our hearts.

October 3

"Make it a rule of life never to regret and never look back. Regret is an appalling waste of energy; you can't build on it; it's only good for walling in."
                                            -Katherine Mansfield

What a great rule to live by! I gave up the I should have's a long time ago. As they say, "Don't should on yourself."

I am thankful that I have been guided to where I am today.

Being a part of the Beauty Industry is something I'm proud of and it has given me focus. If we search for excellence in whatever we choose, we will find it.

When we count our blessings and look to the future, success will surely be ours.

"For Today We'll Find A Way" *to remember that wherever we are, is where we need to be, then we will move forward.*

October 4

"Nothing is obvious to the uninformed."
-Carole Lyden Smith

My daughter, Kelly, dated a nice young man for three years. When he bought her an engagement ring, her mood changed. She was anxious and seemed unsure and unhappy. She felt safe with him.

We had a heart to heart talk. Kelly felt he would make a good father, and she liked him, and he was also her best friend. My advise was, "Kelly you have to make up your own mind. Make sure you have a passion for him too, because marriage is hard enough."

Kelly has extremely high values and standards. She returned the ring and will find her soul mate when the time is right.

"For Today We'll Find A Way" *to approach our relationships with deep passion and caring, to go the distance.*

October 5

"Let our little kids out to play." -Carole Lyden Smith

There's a little kid inside each of us. Do you remember how easy it was to learn, when we were little? To learn to ski isn't as fearful at three as it is at thirty-three.

When we do recognize the child within, we can make light of tasks that would have seemed difficult before.

My little godson, Danny, is two years old. To look at the world through his eyes is so much fun. To play Ninja Turtles with a chair cushion for a shell is more fun for me, than it is for him. My little Donnatello is so precious, and brings out the little kid in me.

"For Today We'll Find A Way" to look to little children for some guidance in how to let go.

October 6

"Clarity leads to power."   *-Carole Lyden Smith*

Is it very clear in your mind and on paper what you really want? Have you signed the paper with your goals on it to validate them? Have you dated it? Have you set your target dates?

Deep down in my heart, I want you to feel the power of getting your goals met. The victory is overwhelming. Are you clear? The point of power is now.

As Dr. Lew says, "Could they play the Super Bowl with no goal posts?"

It is very clear to me that when you visualize the things you want, they will appear. All you have to believe, is you deserve to have them.

"For Today We'll Find A Way" *to be perfectly clear on our goals and our point of power is NOW!*

October 7

"The hardest thing in the world is to think; that's why so few do it."   -Henry Ford

Choosing our professions shows how creative we are.
How many people choose to change destinies? Haven't you felt the changes we have made in peoples lives?
Maybe you have a client like my client, Pat. She works in our town restaurant and knows everyone. She comes by the salon and hangs out for the afternoon, and we exchange stories. Pat is a redhead with beautiful thick hair, due to our color and retail products. She has grown into a confident woman. She has also sent us so many clients because when someone admires her hair, she gives them one of our cards.

"For Today We'll Find A Way" *to be thinkers, shakers and doers. Our point of power is NOW!*

October 8

"You can be free without being creative, but you can't be creative without being free."
— Carole Lyden Smith

All my life, my family has called me a free spirit. I have always gone the distance, when I believed in something.

I believe if you read affirmation books each morning to start your day, you will feel better. If we feel better and better by doing so, isn't is worth the fifteen minutes each day? My fellow professionals, this is a recipe for life that really works.

Depression and frustration are in my past. Peace and serenity are my future.

"For Today We'll Find A Way" to guide our creativity to set ourselves free. We are all in this together. Peace be with you.

October 9

"Don't forget - self worth is more important than other worth."   -Carole Lyden Smith

Deep down, what do you think will bring you happiness? Is it peace in your heart and soul? Is it finding your own serenity? Is it the love of another? Don't you think it takes peace within, before we'll ever find happiness?

We have to bring out the child within and really nurture them. We are usually told everything we do is wrong as children, and very few times, what we've done right. Let's take one step at a time to reassure ourselves that there are no mistakes. Every life experience has brought us to where we are today.

You are an important part of the tapestry of our universe. Let's all give of ourselves, and support each other through the good times and bad.

"For Today We'll Find A Way" *to show self worth is being in sync with nature.*

October 10

"All suffering is the result of infringement of universal principles."   *-Jacquelyn Small*

Each time I feel suffering, whether emotional or physical, I believe in my heart, I have caused it myself. When we all quit blaming other people, places, or things for our stress, the answers will come easier.

We all have to go through some pain to get where we are going. No one's journey is painless. No matter how rich or how poor, we all have some personal pain to *grow* through. If we learn what it is we need to learn, then the pain wasn't in vain.

Instead of beating others down, or feeling jealousy, anger and unhappiness, why don't we learn to love each other in spite of each other's shortcomings?

"For Today We'll Find A Way" *to look at what's right with each other.*

October 11

"The only failure is the failure to participate."
-Carole Lyden Smith

Have you ever known someone so afraid of making the wrong decisions, that they can't seem to make any decisions at all?

My dear friend is that kind of person. He's had the same car for twenty years. He could never make up his mind on what kind of a house to buy, so he rents. He's never been married, and avoids serious relationships. His loyalty to his close friends is impeccable, and he is loving in his own way.

He looks at me like I'm from outer space, because my decisions just seem to come to me. If it's meant to be, it just works; anyway, what's the worst that could happen?

The fun, is in the participation and challenge.

"For Today We'll Find A Way" *to see there are no mistakes.*

October 12

"What I don't like in someone else is unresolved in me."　　　　　　　　*-Carole Lyden Smith*

Have you ever been so frustrated with someone, that you didn't know how to handle it, so you got angry?

I spent a lot of angry years because I wanted this perfect life and perfect family. In the process, I'm sure I alienated a lot of people.

Hey kids, there is a better way. It's actually quite funny - as we get healthier, so do the people around us! As long as I exist, I want to encourage others to find the peace I have been so very lucky to acquire.

If we give away our knowledge and caring, it comes back a hundred times over. If not, where is our personal growth?

"For Today We'll Find A Way" *to find what's right within, and focus on it.*

October 13

"Many of us spend half our time wishing for things we could have, if we didn't spend half our time wishing."   *-Alexander Woolcott*

Our industry has lost many talented, creative people because they didn't take the right steps to build a clientele.

How many new stylists come in and sit in their chair wishing and hoping? Personality is the number one reason that clients stick with a stylist. How much of an impression do you leave with a new client?

We send our clients a postcard, when they're due for a cut. New clients receive $5 off their next visit, $3 off their next two visits and $2 off the next two visits. After six visits they are hooked, hopefully, not only on your service, but on your personality.

"For Today We'll Find A Way" *to go that extra mile for our clients and success will be ours.*

October 14

"Laws of nature do not make exceptions for nice people. A bullet has no conscience; neither does a malignant tumor good people get sick and get hurt as much as anyone."   -Harold S. Kushner

Have you ever promised to style a client's hair if she died? Well, I did. She neglected to tell me, she had cancer.

My partner, Marilyn, and I arrived at our local funeral home. The funeral director's son (a friend and client of mine) asked, "Are you afraid?" We said, "No." He said, "There's salt all over your face from the margueritas." We all laughed and relaxed. Dorothy had baby fine hair. I said, "Hold her up, Jimmy, so I can do the back." "He said no one does the back." I said, "She's not going to heaven with half her hair done. With lots of spray and a curling iron, she looked beautiful.

We didn't feel emotional, until later, when we saw her family and their sorrow.

"For Today We'll Find A Way" *to fulfill our client's every wish.*

October 15

"Thought is creative."   -Carole Lyden Smith

My brother, Rick, is a policeman and always looks at the funny side of things. He was on a call, a raccoon in someone's garbage. They use a hot pepper spray to frighten the raccoon away. He used it as directed, and the varmint ran off and justice, once again, prevailed.

Rick said nature called, and he went to the washroom but forgot to wash his hands first. He then went on his way. Later, he stopped someone that was speeding. As he looked at the person's license, he started burning down below. He yelled, "You're free to go," and tossed back his license. Rick ran off to his patrol car and hurried to the next washroom.

I'm sure the guy with the lead foot is still wondering how come he was so lucky.

"For Today We'll Find A Way" *to be as creative as Rick and be able to laugh at ourselves.*

October 16

"A seed thought is an idea whose time has come that takes hold and changes our reality."
-Jacquelyn Small

I'd like to plant a seed thought for you today. Never settle for less than, you know in your heart, that life is worth.

A great inspirational, plant-a-seed friend, is Lynn (L.B.) Badessa. She is the original find-a-wayer. She encouraged me with my desire to write and helped me plant many seeds along the way.

My network, in making my book happen, is just people I have gotten to be friendly with.

We all have our own network, if we utilize it.

"For Today We'll Find A Way" *to plant the seeds for our future.*

October 17

"The body and soul knows: only our minds can lie."
-Jacquelyn Small

When you know deep down that what you're doing is right it is the best high you can imagine. We are all searching to be *happy*. The answers are within us all.

We could find world peace, if we could each take the time to find our own peace. Do you know how lucky we are to be in an industry that can afford us, not only the material things, but the opportunity to make others feel good?

Let's open up the matrix of our minds and dig deep down to make honest decisions about our future.

"For Today We'll Find A Way" *to reach deep down and allow your body and soul will guide you.*

October 18

"No one comes into my pathway by accident."
-Jacquelyn Small

We are all brought together to learn from each other. My life has been guided by so many wonderful people. As I've said before, when we're ready, the teacher appears.

Amber came into my life as a client when she was in junior high. Her hair was either a rainbow of colors or black, covering her eyes. She was searching to find herself. At seventeen, she started working for us as a nail tech. Acceptance is a major part of our team spirit. We are all different, on different journeys. Amber is now graduating from Pivot Point, and will be a member of our design team. She has grown into a positive young woman who knows where she's going.

"For Today We'll Find A Way" *to be aware of the paths that cross ours.*

October 19

"The first step forward is a step back."
-Carole Lyden Smith

I used to carry three different brands of color in my salon. I didn't feel confident with any of them. I now carry one complete line that is easy to understand and use. It's based on a level system and makes color easy.

We have a distributor of hair-styling portfolios who calls on us regularly. His name is John. He told us that he has never called on a salon that does as much color work as we do. He is so confident, he brings his wife, Vicki, in for color.

For all you young stylists out there, don't be afraid. The more color work you do the easier it becomes. We like to think we've colored our clients worlds a little brighter.

"For Today We'll Find A Way" *to take a step back so we can move forward with direction.*

October 20

"Victimhood is a myth that only leads to powerlessness."   *-Jacquelyn Small*

Have you ever had a friend that was always the victim? My friend is a very loving person, but she always comes out the victim. At work, her bosses don't understand her. She gravitates towards addictive personalities in her relationships. She's unmarried, and a mom. Unless she grows beyond the role of a victim, she will, in turn teach her child the same thing.

When we learn to respect ourselves, and realize we are worth the effort to change, we can leave powerlessness in the past.

Recovery can bring some pain, but if not for ourselves, why not pave a better way for our children?

"For Today We'll Find A Way" *to have respect for ourselves.*

October 21

"Love points the way for us to express our human nature; truth makes these ways possible."
-Jacquelyn Small

Looking for love in all the wrong places was how I can describe my means of looking for a mate. Life as a hairdresser leaves us emotionally spent on a lot of occasions. We can financially support ourselves but what I've always looked for, is emotional support.

I've always thought I had to be everything. The best wife, mother, stylist and salon owner. When we take the time to be the best person we can be, the rest is easy.

I always like to start my day by asking for some divine guidance, and somehow, I'm always where I need to be.

"For Today We'll Find A Way" to remember, love is easy to find when we give love in all areas of our lives.

October 22

"In personality we are many, in 'essence' we are one."   *-Jacquelyn Small*

When I think of all the personalities that I have come to love, in our industry alone, it overwhelms me.

The Midwest Show comes to mind with the altieri brothers, Sabino and Visions. Jordan pulls all the shows together as one. What an extravaganza!

We are all there to share in each others lives, to make even one minute in the salon easier for each other.

We all have the ability to put each other at ease and give one another confidence. We are all an intricate part of this collage of life. Why not participate to the fullest?

"For Today We'll Find A Way" *to love one another, share our feelings and let each other know how important we all are.*

October 23

"You have forgotten yourself and that is your only fault."   *-Jacquelyn Small*

Early in my career, I was so busy people pleasing, that I forgot the most valuable thing I have to give - myself. When I share my feelings with others, it nurtures me. I know the more focused I become, the more in tune I am with who I am.

What does intimacy mean to you? My dear friend Carol Lyden Smith shared, *In To Me See,* are we ready yet to let others see into us?

Whatever the reasons in my past were, shame, hurt, insecurity or fear, I am now ready to trust and in the process, heal myself.

"For Today We'll Find A Way" *to nurture our child within and not be afraid to share intimacies with our friends.*

October 24

"Addiction is non-growth - a way of being stuck in the past. If a natural urge has been thwarted, addictions set in. Therefore, addiction can be viewed as blocked creative energy."
-Jacquelyn Small

It's amazing how much creative energy we all possess. If we can get past any signs of addictive behavior, we can increase our creativity.

I am so thankful to be able to recognize my addictions, because many people live in a state of denial.

I am also thankful that I don't miss alcohol, and the need to try to control The operative word is *try* because we really have no control over anything or anyone but ourselves.

"For Today We'll Find A Way" *for our creative energy to flow.*

October 25

"We can recognize an addiction by its lack of life-giving qualities. It drains us of our prime energy, the energy to self-create."   -Jacquelyn Small

When we are caught up in a life of addiction, whether it be drinking, drugs, eating, relationships or work we lose our perspective. It drains us and our personal growth suffers. Sickness and despair are a big part of the addictive world.

When we make a conscious effort to grow through addictive behavior, it will be well worth the victory. Every day, new doors open up for me. I don't think I would have recognized opportunity when I was into my addiction, because it consumes you.

I am so thankful for my life now. I am free from control. I am guided by my higher power.

"For Today We'll Find A Way" *to make the call so we can be free of addiction.*

October 26

"Our inner state of mind determines our outer life, not the other way around."   -Jacqueline Small

Do we fill our minds with good thoughts? Do we tell ourselves we will succeed? Do we love unconditionally?

As I look back over the past four years, I feel a new person has emerged. It feels so good to be focused.

It amazes me that no matter what problems I've had, they are now non-existent. Our business is unique in the sense that we have staggered work hours and we deal with emotions.

Depression and uncertainty is in the past. I am ready for my future, whatever it brings. I've let go of controlling, and opened myself up for positive guidance in harmony with the universe.

"For Today We'll Find A Way" *to focus on the positives and find our peace.*

October 27

"Because we can change our thinking, we can change our lives. Heaven and hell are nothing but states of consciousness." -Jacquelyn Small

As I look back at where I was ten years ago and where I am today, I just smile to myself and a good warm feeling floods through me. I know how very lucky I am.

What has changed? Only my state of consciousness. I am a person at peace and harmony professionally and personally. My heaven is here and now. I would hope that each and every one of you will find your own serenity.

"For Today We'll Find A Way" *to heaven, by allowing positive thinking.*

October 28

"Self-knowledge is knowledge of the 'Spirit' and does not belong to any sect or religious group."
-Jacqueline Small

Jan, a dear friend and client, asked me to be a patient at Loyola Dental School for her son Frank. I needed a root canal, so I was referred to Dr. Gene, soon to be a certified endodontist.

Gene and I got to talking. He shared his feelings about his mother, Gloria, who has terminal cancer. The compassion in his heart showed in his eyes. I told Gene as long as he and his four sisters live and breath, a part of his mom would always be alive. For what are we, but a part of our parents?

I also told Gene that my daughter, Kelly, could guide him to a salon in our area that specializes in wigs for people who receive chemo.

"For Today We'll Find A Way" *to realize we cross each other's paths to help, guide and nurture.*

October 29

"Trust the instinct to the end, though you can render no reason."   *-Ralph Waldo Emerson*

Our natural instinct can help us in all aspects of our lives.

I believe fate brings us together and instinct causes us to be in the right place at the right time.

I've worked with different distributors, while working hair shows. There's a man that is in charge of a large operation in the midwest. His name is Bill, and he always has a smile on his face and a positive attitude. The sales consultants genuinely seem to enjoy working for him. He seems to have a lot of instinct in running these big shows. Through the help of his team, they really pull it all together.

"For Today We'll Find A Way" *to trust our instincts.*

October 30

"Nowhere can a man find a quieter or more untroubled retreat than in his own soul."
                                                        -Marcus Aurelius

Each and every morning, I am so thankful to take quiet time to myself. My going within has helped me discover my own peace.

We are all in such a fast paced business, with so many irons in the fire, it helps to focus each morning and be thankful for the day ahead.

If we all just set our ego aside, and be humble enough to love one another, success and peace will come.

The more we give, the more we get.

"For Today We'll Find A Way" *to take the time to discover who we really are. Be happy to be an intricate part of this great big universe.*

October 31

"One word frees us from all the weight and pain of life: that word is love."   *-Sophocles*

Halloween has always been one of my favorite holidays. I guess I could be myself, and no one would think I'm weird. Everyone in the salon dresses up.

This year, Cari was a lion, her makeup was excellent. Stacey was Raggedy Ann. Kelly and I were Hershey kisses, she was plain and I was almond (kind of a nut, right?).

After work, we went for dinner at a restaurant and lounge. After dinner, we went into the bar for a contest. Cari won first place and got $100. Stacey won second for $50 and Kelly and I won third for $25. We gave cards to all runner ups for a complimentary visit to our salon; network everywhere you go.

"For Today We'll Find A Way" to let your little kid out for a day of fun. Happy Halloween!!!

November 1

"Breakdown of the family unit is the breakdown of the world."   -Carole Lyden Smith

With the high rate of divorce and despair, the family unit is at great risk. Whether there's one parent or two, it's important that we reassure each member of the family they are very important and wonderful.

If we feed our children negative messages, we will have negative children that grow up to be negative adults.

With all the distractions our world presents, TV, VCR's and staggered work schedules and everyone running in different directions, isn't it time to make time to be together?

If we want world peace, we must start with peace from within. If we have focus and a good sense of self, we will be able to pass this on to our families.

"For Today We'll Find A Way" to program our lives for peace.

November 2

"You can have it all. Thank you."
-Carole Lyden Smith

You really can have it all! Choosing the company of products you wish to support, is a very important decision.

Is the company (retail and service products) you support, there to help you learn to run your business efficiently? How to understand yourself? How to get clients and keep them? How to satisfy your own needs and wants? How to establish where your expertise is in our industry? How about co-op advertising?

The company I chose ten years ago, does all these things. Small salon owners need all the help they can get to make their money go further.

"For Today We'll Find A Way" *to have it all!*

November 3

"We raise our children exactly like we were raised until we make a conscious decision to change."
   -Carole Lyden Smith

I'm so thankful my focus has changed, if not only for myself, but for my two beautiful loving children, Kelly and Jamie.

I worried so much when they were growing up, making sure they had designer clothes, best schools, best loving nanny (Nancy Burda) and every toy that they uttered they might want.

Now I realize, that they already had everything. They had a mother with a find-a-way attitude which prepared her to change the dysfunctions of the past. The only thing that kept me diligent on my search for peace, is my love for them.

Our journey gets better with every bit of growth we encounter.

"For Today We'll Find A Way" *to see how important the young people are in our lives. Let's give them loving guidance.*

November 4

"Happiness comes of the capacity to feel deeply, to enjoy simply, to think freely, to risk life, to be needed."   -Storm Jameson

It truly amazes me how strong people must be to move to a new country. God Bless them for their enthusiasm for a new way.

When I moved to Las Vegas, I was surprised how devastating it can be to relocate. My cousins Bobby and Amy were the emotional support which helped me adjust.

I made many friends in Las Vegas with whom I continue to feel a strong bond. Although miles apart, we are still very close and remain in touch. I now visit Terry and Brooks on Lake Erie near Cleveland. Cheryl, Bill, Denise and Terry remain in Las Vegas. Margo has moved to the Chicago area near me.

"For Today We'll Find A Way" *to understand that risk can bring love and friendship.*

November 5

"You can be healed (of depression) if everyday you begin the first thing in the morning to consider how you can bring a real joy to someone else. If you can stick to this for two weeks, you will no longer need therapy."   -Alfred Adler

How long does it take to make someone feel good? Send a note to someone who's a little down, whether it be an old friend, a client or a co-worker. It's such a good feeling to know someone cares.

In my experience, the kindness I show others has come back to me one hundred times over.

I have a dear friend, Cheryl, who kids me and asks, "Colleen, how do you meet all the nice people?" I always tell her, "I'm just really lucky."

"For Today We'll Find A Way" *to take the time to make others feel good and we will feel great.*

November 6

"The first step forward is the hardest...The next starts the momentum."   -Carole Lyden Smith

It's a funny thing. Ten years ago, I didn't have a clue where I wanted to be today, other than to be successful.

It all started with a dream, and step by step, inch by inch, the last ten years have been a wonderful experience in personal and professional growth. Once the momentum starts, it's amazing how things just start getting better and better.

Once we make a conscious effort to change, set down our goals and the purpose of our goals, it all starts to happen.

I write my daily goals on my mirror, and affirm them each morning.

"For Today We'll Find A Way" *to take a giant step forward.*

November 7

"Friendship is like a bank account. You can't continue to draw on it without making deposits."
-Bits and Pieces

Each time I work a show, I realize how many wonderful friends I've made in the last ten years.

Each show takes so much team effort. The deep caring and love of our industry is what carries us through.

When our feet hurt so bad we feel as if we've taken our last step, we hobble to our rooms, spray our feet with Instacure over and over, until we fall asleep. We get up at 4:30 a.m. to give the show our all, just one more day.

"For Today We'll Find A Way" *to let our momentum grow through each other.*

November 8

"To get nowhere, follow the crowd." -Anonymous

Each of us lives with a different set of values. What are the rules we live by? These are thoughts that have gone through my mind as I started preparing a salon handbook. This lets future and present employees understand what is important to me, and also the values I live by.

What makes our company different from the next is the standards we project.

Our salon values are as follows:
- Friendly motivated manner.
- Team member.
- Kind.
- Honest.
- A find-a-wayer.
- Internally focused for success.

"For Today We'll Find A Way" *to work independently toward our goals.*

November 9

"When a small child...I thought that success spelled happiness. I was wrong, happiness is like a butterfly which appears and delights us for one brief moment, but soon flits away." -Anna Pavlova

Pulling together the loose ends, I have spent the last five years bringing it all into focus.

- Deep in my soul, I have found peace and serenity.
- I have been able to focus all my endeavors through my spiritual focus.
- My excessive personality brings happiness instead of dysfunction.
- My children I love unconditionally.
- I am in the process of redesigning my body.
- I work everyday on healthy relationships.
- I have found success in the business I love.

"For Today We'll Find A Way" *to have our butterfly touch us daily.*

November 10

"Life is a process, not an emergency."   *-Midwife*

When Carole Lyden Smith shared the story of the birth of her beautiful granddaughter, my daughter Kelly and I were so overwhelmed, we started to cry.

Little Carolyn was brought into the world with the stereo playing "Lazar" in Carole and Don's home. She was shown love from the very moment of her arrival.

Her daughter's midwife suggested filling the house with flowers, and having a great banquet for this wonderful occasion.

If we show our little ones there's no emergency with life, just loving, guidance and positive energy, they'll grow up with high self esteem.

"For Today We'll Find A Way" *to nurture each other in our process of life.*

November 11

"I long to accomplish a great and noble task, but it is my chief duty to accomplish small tasks as if they were great and noble."   -Helen Keller

I guess the great strength Helen Keller has given us, is there are no obstacles, if we know not to limit ourselves.

Each day, as you walk into the salon, try and do each task with love and assurance. Be happy for the goodness you bring into everyone's lives.

You and I, together, can bring world peace by finding peace with each other.

Imagine all people in the beauty industry with their hands linked together. How many times would we go around the world?

"For Today We'll Find A Way" to perform each small task today with peace and our day will be great and noble.

November 12

"You must learn to promote yourself."
-Carole Lyden Smith

What have you done as a stylist or as an owner to promote business?

Wishing and hoping won't get us there.

We offered to do a fashion show which was sponsed by one of the churches in our town. We all pitched in and cut, colored and glossed the models' hair. They looked beautiful walking down the runway. Each time the announcer said, "Hair Shapers," and told what kind of cut and color were used, the girls beamed. Teamwork! We can *all* be platform artists in our own way. We also distributed samples of hair and skin care products with discount cards usable on their first visit to our salon.

We also distributed products and services for door prizes. We reached 100 potential new clients!

"For Today We'll Find A Way" *to create our own excitement.*

November 13

"Your future is in your hands according to the way you think and act."   -Carole Lyden Smith

Visualization can bring all our goals home. Have we written down the type of salon we want and its contents? As we visualize the things we'd like in this salon, it will begin to be real. What kind of equipment do you want, what color, how many stations?

My next move will be into my own building, so as my salon grows, it will be on my own property. I will have a nice condo upstairs, so instead of two mortgages, I have one beautiful building for business and home.

I truly love this business of making people feel good. We are so lucky to be at an intricate part of our clients' lives.

"For Today We'll Find A Way" *to make our lists, and check them twice. Our future is NOW.*

November 14

"You have to walk the talk."   -*Dennis Lubin*

I prefer to think the world is a better place due to the love of our fellow salon professionals.

As a salon owner, I feel the most valuable thing I can do in guiding young stylists, is follow the same rules I expect them to follow. We all learn by example. If we want enthusiastic employees, we have to show enthusiasm.

Everyone needs to feel needed. When someone does something nice, commend them for it. If we always remember what it's like to be the new kid on the block, we will reassure our co-workers how important they are to our team.

"For Today We'll Find A Way" *to show each other the love and respect it takes to build a winning team.*

November 15

"The most powerful thing, is what I say to myself and believe!"　　　　-Carole Lyden Smith

Do we start out each day with a quiet time to collect our thoughts? This time is the most important part of my day. I like to meditate and read my daily affirmation books to set my mood for the day.

We all have the power to make our lives positive. In order to do so, we must take one positive step at a time.

Do we believe in our hearts we are worthy of success? Do we think we deserve it? We must make a conscious effort to change; once we make the decision, we are half way there.

The only way I see to get a grasp on success, is to give it away. Share all you know to help the next person. It feels great!

"For Today We'll Find A Way" to help everyone we can today!

November 16

"The faultfinder will find faults even in paradise."
                        -Henry David Thoreau

Have you ever worked with a stylist that complained from morning till night? They never get the good clients, their hours are the worst, they hate salon meetings and not only is their life at work miserable, but they never get the dates, their parents don't understand them and they never get any breaks!

Now tell me, would you want someone like that to work with? It is so much nicer to build on life's pluses rather than the minuses.

We all have the ability to be happy. We must go within to find our way.

"For Today We'll Find A Way" *to go within to find our positive mental attitude.*

November 17

"Synergy promotes wholeness."
-Carole Lyden Smith

Synergy means total cooperation and teamwork that produces optimum results.

If our salons are synergized, it means that, instead of each person working individually on their own, we work together, to make the whole more powerful and successful.

Think of how a fine surgical team works together. Each doing their part to ensure the wellness of the patient. What no one person can achieve on their own, when linked together, they have the strength to achieve miracles.

When we have a team that works, with the strength of one another, all things are possible. From manufacturer, to distributor, to sales consultant, to salon owner, to stylist, to consumer - Total Teamwork!

"For Today We'll Find A Way" *to synergize our team to wholeness.*

November 18

"Imagination is the wings that thought rides upon in order to produce a creation."
                                    -Carole Lyden Smith

Cari, one of my stylists, is a very special girl. She has really grown as a professional and as a person.

She's been with us three years, and met her fiancee, Brad, in our salon. She always said she'd never date her clients, so instead she's marrying him.

This morning, Cari was baptized into Peace Church, which is two blocks down from our salon. Of course this was a tender moment for me, and I was all teary eyed.

Do you believe yet, that there are reasons we are all brought together? I feel every moment we share in each other's lives has meaning.

"For Today We'll Find A Way" to spread our wings so our imagination can produce a creation.

November 19

"The point of Power is in the now."
-Carole Lyden Smith

As we walk into our salons today, what is our point of power? Are our goals set? What new service will we offer each and every client? It has been said, "Ask and you shall receive." Believe me, there's so much truth to that.

If you want a raise in salary, create one. *We* have found, that when we suggest a perm or color, if a client doesn't get it that day, usually they will on the next visit. Remember to note on their client card what you suggested and highlight it for easy referral.

"For Today We'll Find A Way" *to make our point of Power now!*

November 20

"You can have it all!!"   *-Carole Lyden Smith*

Why do some stylists make two hundred a week and some make two thousand a day?

Do you really think it's because they cut hair better? I think not. It's because they believe they're worth it.

Do you look in the mirror and tell yourself you're the best? Does it sound silly to you? It sounded strange to me, at first, too. We must affirm the things we want, and we will surely have them.

We must reprogram all the negative garbage into positive affirmations. Write down your goals. Make sure you write down the purpose for each, and reaffirm them each day.

Example: I will finish my book. Purpose: to make others feel as good as I do.

"For Today We'll Find A Way" *to have it all.*

November 21

"To different minds, the same world is hell and a heaven."   *Ralph Waldo Emerson*

Can you imagine how heavy someone's burden is, who has to deal with prejudice? Whether it's color, religion, ethnic origin or sexual preference.

Prejudice means opinions formed without basis. None of us have a choice what color we are or what family we are born into.

When a person makes fun of another person, have they really taken the time to put themselves in the other person's shoes? Human kindness can make the difference in another person's life and it doesn't cost a penny.

Prejudice can not only cause pain but could cost us what could have been a nice friendship.

"For Today We'll Find A Way" *to be open minded and kind. We can make the first move to end prejudice!*

November 22

"Progress is a process."   *-Carole Lyden Smith*

When I started on my positive journey of personal growth, it brought out a lot of hidden feelings which frightened me. I had learned to stuff my feelings for so long, to feel, meant to be vulnerable, and it truly terrified me.

In the process of making progress, we must take one step at a time. So many of us want to be perfect, but it's so simple, if we let go, we will see that we already are.

If I can give you one positive thought for today, it's *progress not perfection*. Give yourself a break! You will get there and find your own peace.

"For Today We'll Find A Way" *to make positive progress.*

November 23

"Courage is moving forward through fear. Reaching victory is so sweet."   -Carole Lyden Smith

When my daughter, Kelly, was sixteen years old, I sent her out to look for a house. I gave her the criteria: what we could afford, what we had for a down payment, a home within her school district and what style I'd like the house to be.

The first realtor, Rob Shade, who would talk with her, is from whom we bought our beautiful townhome.

I had no doubt she could do it, so therefore, she had no doubt. She really has a much better expertise for shopping than I do. Give the power to someone that likes the job.

"For Today We'll Find A Way" *to find our own truths. Our recovery can bring us victory.*

November 24

"The point of power is now!"   -Carole Lyden Smith

After taking Carole's Experiential Learning Class, I realized, that all we have to do is open our hearts and our minds to what we really want, and it will be ours.

We learned that intimacy means "In to me see." This has always been an issue for me. I'm learning to open up and share my feelings.

We have so much to offer each other as professionals. Why not open up, and we'll all be stronger?

We did an exercise, to pick a partner by using eye contact. Ralph, a sales consultant, was my pick. It truly amazed me. I am learning to trust my instincts. I have found a good friend in Ralph - genuine, kind, honest and spiritual.

"For Today We'll Find A Way" *to see our point of power is now!!*

November 25

"Change is the only thing for certain."
-Carole Lyden Smith

As we look back over the years, to see what has brought us to where we are, whether good or bad, let's be thankful for learning that to change is an essential part of personal fulfillment.

Our industry is one, in which the only limits for us, are in our own minds.

We are at a time in which service and personal image are what one's clients are looking for. We don't just dress hair anymore. We build self esteem and confidence in guiding our clients to be all that they can be.

"For Today We'll Find A Way" to greet change with open arms.

November 26

"I can't keep what I have unless I give it away."
-Twelve Step Program

The most important thing we can give each other is love.

My son, Jamie, is frustrated himself by control. When he gets angry at his girlfriend Kristine, and looks to me for answers, all I can say is, "Jamie, just love her without trying to control her. There is no room for buts or why can't she."

Why do we frustrate ourselves with trying to change everyone around us, when the answers are within us?

Kristine and Jamie are growing closer each day in recovery. I know in my heart, they will find the peace in their program and give Zachary, their son, all he needs to be healthy and happy - LOVE.

"For Today We'll Find A Way" *to see the more love we give away the more we get back.*

November 27

"What a man really has, is what is in him. What is outside him, should be a matter of no importance."
                                            -Oscar Wilde

My children's father is a special kind of man. He adopted my son, Jamie, from my first marriage, and has always been a loving father. We had Kelly and his love of being a father flourished. Andy loves his children equally, and tries to have their best interest at heart. Although we are divorced, he is still my very dear friend.

When I see Andy with our grandson Zak, I see how much love he has to give. We are still family.

When a marriage doesn't work out, remember, it wasn't all bad, and we grow from our experience.

"For Today We'll Find A Way" *to look inside, to see the goodness in others.*

November 28

"Positive thoughts produce positive results. Negative thoughts produce negative results."
            -Carole Lyden Smith

I have a dear friend who shall remain nameless for obvious reasons.

As a young man, he got involved in the wrong way of life. His friends were gangsters. His relationships were bad, and he also went through drug addiction. Out of these negative years, he learned that all he got was negative results.

He now owns a legitimate business, is a good father, and knows in his heart that honesty *is* the best policy.

"For Today We'll Find A Way" to feed our minds with positive thoughts and we will have positive results.

November 29

"Advice is what we ask for when we already know the answer but wish we didn't."   -Erica Jong

In the past, when I was troubled about something, I would ask people for advice. Maybe I was looking for an easier way or a miracle.

Now, I go within for solutions, because we have all the answers inside. Once we have centered ourselves, all we need is a little quiet time, and the solutions appear.

So many times our clients ask for advice, and we can listen and ask them, "How do *you* feel about it?" Most of the time, they have already figured out how to achieve the solution.

"For Today We'll Find A Way" *to see that our own experience is our best teacher.*

November 30

"I'm not going to limit myself just because people won't accept the fact that I can do something else."
                                              -Dolly Parton

Hairdressing is at the center of my soul. What other profession can give me the success and peace that this one has given me?

My ultimate goal would be to reach out and teach young stylists how to build their career through personal focus. Not only will focus help them professionally, but personally as well.

Our journeys are not over until our last breath. Why not build strength in our industry by helping each other.

"For Today We'll Find A Way" *to reach for the stars and be inspired by the challenges before us. We will succeed!*

December 1

"What I don't like in someone else - is unresolved in me."   -Carole Lyden Smith

Let's think of someone we have had a lot of conflict with. Does this person mirror an image of something in ourselves we don't like?

When a person does hateful things, it only reassures me, that the thing they hate the most is themselves. How very sad for them.

If we live with ridicule and negativity as children, we grow up to be insecure adults with low self esteem who act out on others. We can change at any age, whether six or sixty. We have the strength within to make positive changes to find our serenity.

"For Today We'll Find A Way" *so that when we encounter people we don't like, we will look at them and learn , then let go and love unconditionally.*

December 2

"The greatest men this nation has ever known have always been quick to acknowledge their dependence on a power greater than themselves, and quick to seek aid from the power."
                                        -Norman Vincent Peale

Each of us has our own power source to tap.

I am so thankful I have found my own focus. The answers are already in us all. The first step forward is a step back to refocus. We must all find courage to be honest with ourselves.

Let's make a list of what would make us happy. To achieve our goals they must be written down and very clear.
- Spiritual.
- Personal.
- Professional.

To really make the commitment, document your goals and sign them and then refer to them daily.

"For Today We'll Find A Way" *to have our higher power guide us to reach our goals.*

December 3

"To be somebody you must last."   *-Ruth Gordon*

When I was a young child, I knew in my heart, that I had a special knack to make people realize their own potential. I have gone through many personal changes in the discovery of who I really am. The bottom line is to go the distance.

Ruth Gordon has always been one of my favorite actresses because she never gives up. She looks for the challenges her life brings.

When I was thirty, I went to a Ruth Gordon Festival with my dear friend Bill Murphy, and we laughed through all her movies. It will always be a very special day in my memory.

"For Today We'll Find A Way" *to look for the special Bill Murphy and Ruth Gordon's in your life.*

December 4

"Flowers grow out of dark moments."
                    -Corita Kent

When we're going through a dark moment in our lives, and the hurts are hard to bear, remember some good always comes out to guide us.

When our family lost my seventeen year old sister Carrie, we were all devastated and sick inside. It took us literally years to heal our aching hearts.

Our family is so close, and we take the time to be together. We are so thankful to have each other.

I used to be so busy running with friends and doing things I thought were important, but the reality is we must make the time to be with our families.

"For Today We'll Find A Way" *to reflect on how our flower gardens are growing, and look towards the light.*

December 5

"Belief consists in accepting the affirmations of the soul; unbelief in denying them."
                                                    -Ralph Waldo Emerson

Humor is always a part of my life. One of the most important lessons that I've learned is to be able to laugh at myself.

I called my friend, Tom, who works for our local Friendly Shopper Newspaper. I told him I wanted to put in an ad to find a hairdresser. The ad said, "Looking for a motivated, happy hairdresser to add to our Hair Shaper Team, must have PMA." Tom asked, "Are you sure you want someone with that?" I asked, "With what?" He was thinking of PMS.

The ingredient that we must have to succeed as a professional, is a positive mental attitude.

"For Today We'll Find A Way" to affirm our souls.

December 6

"If you knew how often I said to myself: to hell with everything, to hell with everybody. I've done my share, let others do theirs now, enough, enough, enough."   *-Golda Meir*

If you are a go getter, it's hard to understand people with little or no motivation.

Be thankful for being a mover and a shaker, because we will make the difference.

In the salon, it's always the busy stylists that get things done.

Yes, we all can make life in the salon better by three little rules.
- Be kind.
- Have a good attitude.
- Never give up!

"For Today We'll Find A Way" *to realize when enough is really enough.*

December 7

"Any man can seek revenge, it takes a king or a prince to grant a pardon."   *-Arthur J. Rehrat*

Working in the salon each day, with so many personalities, it can be very frustrating. Moods vary, in most people, daily. Feelings can get hurt easily when so many are working under pressure and in close quarters.

Try and remember it takes a bigger person to let go of ill feelings. Fear makes people react differently, sometimes with anger, a nervous look, or being withdrawn.

The sign of a true professional is not to let it show.

"For Today We'll Find A Way" *to let go, if someone hurts our feelings.*

December 8

"The main dangers in this life are the people who want to change everything or nothing."
                                        -Carole Lyden Smith

The most important thing we can find in our lives is balance. I have an excessive personality, so for me, this isn't easy. I tend to go overboard. So each day I look for balance.

Life in the salon makes it hard to achieve balance. One day it's busy with no room for a break, and the next day may be sporadic with lots of time in our schedules.

If we each work as a team member, we will insure success for everyone.

Remember, if we want to form a good habit, we must practice a new habit for twenty-one days in a row.

"For Today We'll Find A Way" *to make little changes each day, so over all, we will find our own balance.*

December 9

"All it takes is a little willingness."
-Carole Lyden Smith

Victory Beauty Systems has a wonderful education director in the midwest, Pam Koenig. She called me and asked me to help set up models for Jim Jones, a dynamic motivational speaker and haircutter.

It was so enjoyable especially for me. My nephews Matthew and Danny, ages three and two started the show. Then came my brother Rick, nephew Danny, nephew Scot and my son, Jamie. It was not only educational for my staff and myself, but was a fun family day that my brother captured on video, for eternity.

If you have the opportunity to catch Jim Jones in action, he's a sure thing. He also does hands-on workshops in his area or your salon.

"For Today We'll Find A Way" *to see what our motivator is. Love of family and friends is a good beginning.*

December 10

"No one can make you feel inferior without your consent."   *-Eleanor Roosevelt*

In my early days in the salon, I was so afraid of not caring enough for my clients.

A client would come in and tell me all her problems, and I would take it all in and worry about it all week. The next week I would ask, "How is the situation with your husband?" She would reply, "Oh, everything worked out okay."

It took me a few years with a nervous stomach and an ulcer, to realize I give my clients a lot more than a hairdo. I can and do give them confidence in themselves. To give people the strength to believe in themselves, is the greatest gift we have.

"For Today We'll Find A Way" *to understand the strength and confidence we give our clients.*

December 11

"Winning isn't everything, it's the only thing."
-Vince Lombardi

Winning for me has meant the freedom of frustration. I spent so many years worrying about things that really don't matter.

Have you ever had the *what if* syndrome? What if I can't pay this bill? What if I get sick? What if my marriage doesn't work? What if I have a slow week in the salon?

Learn to focus and believe things will take care of themselves.

If I had to give the next generation one piece of advise, it would be to focus yourself and you'll realize, with inner peace, all your situations will be winners.

"For Today We'll Find A Way" *to forgive yourself, focus and realize the best we can do is love and help each other.*

December 12

"There's a period of life when we swallow a knowledge of ourselves and it becomes either good or sour inside."   -Pearl Bailey

Take each day one day at a time, one foot in front of the other, stay on the right path. Find your balance, and believe with your whole being what you are doing is honest and true.

I have let go of the past, and now I feel whole. I've always felt a little like Crusader Rabbit, knowing if I care enough I will make the difference in many lives.

Ten years ago I was depressed and confused. I am thankful for the focus I have found, and the more I can give all of you, the more my wholeness is complete. I know who I am and the goodness we can find together.

"For Today We'll Find A Way" *because it's the first day of the rest of our lives.*

December 13

"I am creating my future right now by the choices I am making and I have a wise self within that will guide me to the next right step. If I will be still and listen."   *-Jacqueline Small*

Can you imagine my excitement the day Arlene Tolin called me from Modern Salon? They were preparing the February 1991 edition, and wanted me to do a perm layout for them.

Arlene said they had called for a list of stylists in the Chicago area, and my name was the one they suggested.

My, how good it feels to be respected and loved by our peers.

I'd like to thank all of my professional family for the confidence they have in me, especially Julie Montean.

"For Today We'll Find A Way" *to go down the right path and my truth will guide me where I need to be.*

December 14

"Cherish your visions and your dreams; as they are the children of your soul, the blueprints of your ultimate achievements."   -Napoleon Hill

All my life I have been lucky enough to understand the importance of networking. My visions and dreams are becoming realities because of the wonderful network of friends that have helped me pull it all together.

Remember, that each and every person you meet is an important part of the tapestry of your life story.

Just as a caterpillar goes into his cocoon and struggles to emerge as a butterfly, we must all struggle to realize our ultimate achievements.

Through clients, friends in the industry, family and a network of caring individuals, I am reaching all of you. In the deepest part of my soul, I believe peace and success can be yours in the same manner.

"For Today We'll Find A Way" *to share ourselves with each other.*

December 15

"Take your life in your own hands and what happens? A terrible thing: no one to blame."
    -Erica Jong

How can we take responsibility for our own lives and our own successes?

UNSUCCESSFUL
- I never get any good clients.
- I only wear old clothes because I don't want to ruin my good ones.
- I'm in no hurry, I have to be here all day.
- I only like the people that are like me.
- I'll keep my blinders on.

SUCCESSFUL
- Build my own clients.
- I dress for success.
- I give good service.
- I love everyone unconditionally.
- I never limit the visions of my future.

"For Today We'll Find A Way" to take credit for our own successes.

December 16

"All of my experiences, including my years of drunkenness, have been perfect. They have afforded me the grounding for understanding human suffering. Now I am prepared for a life of service..."
-Jacqueline Small

If I can share one thing with all of you, it is that we are all on a journey of discovery. In order to have a happy, successful life, we must start with peace in our own hearts.

Sometimes I get overwhelmed with the suffering of others, mostly because I too have suffered, and can remember the despair.

If we all start each morning with a positive focus on how we can help the next person, we will find our peace.

"For Today We'll Find A Way" *to open up our hearts and give freely.*

December 17

"You take a setback and turn it into a comeback."
-Kyle Woods

Haven't we all, as salon owners/operators, had the devastation of losing a favorite designer or a group of designers? I want to share with you, that deep in my soul, I believe there is a reason people come and go in our lives. We have to remember during these times that our journey has been better by sharing the time and by knowing when to let go and get on with life.

My life is quite full, and all the wonderful professionals, that have shared time with me, have helped make the difference in my career.

Thank God for my guidance.

"For Today We'll Find A Way" *to turn our lives over to our higher power.*

December 18

"Transformation does not occur from changes in the world outside us; we create the miracle from within."
                                              -Jacquelyn Small

Why do you get up everyday? Is it for compensation? Here's a method for success my cousin Dan O'Brien taught me.

Compensation - Comp-method

C	ommitment
O	rganization
M	anagement
P	erformance

Today is a gift...there are no guarantees. I get up everyday to have fun and make money. It's no great mystery, the more fun I have, the more money I make.

If you have trouble meeting a goal, go back to your commitment.

"For Today We'll Find A Way" to *"comp"ensate our dedication.*

December 19

"Life must flow harmoniously from experience to experience."   *-Jacqueline Small*

Have you read *Power of the Plus Factor* by Norman Vincent Peale? I got this motivational book for Christmas from our new team member, Blanche. I will be eternally grateful.

We all have the plus factor, whether we choose to recognize it or not. My term for the plus factor is *focus* in my life and I love his book and his theories. He suggests to dream creative dreams, set high and worthwhile goals and take the first decisive step towards your goal.

Then, no matter how long it takes, persist, persevere and hang in there.

"For Today We'll Find A Way" to find your own plus factor. Thanks to Blanche, I've found mine.

December 20

"We can only leave behind us what we have mastered, balanced, or outgrown."
                                                    -Jacqueline Small

Exercise - ugh!!! My weight has always been a sore spot with me. Food has always been my addiction of choice.

I am in the process of redesigning my body. I joined a weight loss program, and the weight is coming off. I also know exercise is the key to permanent weight loss.

Everyone at the salon decided to give me support by going to work out at our town leisure center. All the girls and quite a few of our clients set our for a workout. What could have been a horrible experience was fun, because we tackled it together.

"For Today We'll Find A Way" *to give love and support to each other so we can master this exercise/diet concept.*

December 21

"Man is the sum total of countless influences playing upon him since infancy." -Norman Vincent Peale

Every January, I attend an ACOA retreat at Villa Desdirata. Everyone attending is in a different place on their journey.

My son, Jamie, and his girlfriend, Kris, went this year. It was a dream come true for me to see my son working on his recovery so we can break the chains of the past. His son, Zachary, will have a healthier environment in which to live.

Jamie reacts with anger when his feelings are hurt. He's learning to live one day at a time and to work through his anger.

Remember, we don't pick our parents and they don't pick theirs. We all come with a lot of baggage, and sometimes it hurts our feelings.

"For Today We'll Find A Way" *to see the benefits of recovery are peace and serenity.*

December 22

"Life shrinks or expands in proportion to one's courage."   *-Anais Nin*

Every year, the Sunday before Christmas, some friends and I organize a Christmas party. Santa rides in on his sleigh with a bag of gifts. We began this tradition with my niece, Eileen, my two nephews, Jeff and Andy, and three other young children of friends. When you see those wide eyes, it's worth all the preparation. Now, there's about two hundred children and we hold it at a local health club with Santa, Mrs. Claus, elves and helpers.

My friend, Marsha, and I spend time with these old friends once a year. We've all grown in different directions, but it's nice to get together for this great Christmas gala.

"For Today We'll Find A Way" *to light up the eyes of little children.*

December 23

"In every new experience, happy or sad, there's a need to let go of what WAS. Until we do, we can't appreciate what is."   -Barbara Bartocci

For many years, I carried around excess baggage. I have since learned to let go of the past and be thankful for what is.

In finding my own focus, I realize the most important thing we can do for ourselves is keep our minds open to what our own journey has to offer.

I used to spend most of my time trying to guide others by control. Each of our journeys is very special just by letting it happen one day at a time.

"For Today We'll Find A Way" to let go of what was, so we can appreciate what is.

December 24

"Anyone can sail with a fair breeze. It's when the seas get rough that seamanship, really understanding the sea, counts."
-Norman Vincent Peale

In these times, when we see so many salons closing their doors, we have to be thankful that there are good companies that truly care about our business.

It's never to late to sign up for a Salon Psychology class with Dr. Lew, or Experiential Learning with Carole Lyden Smith. They have given me the courage to make positive changes, so my salon will run efficiently with an enthusiastic team.

Plenty of classes are offered by many different companies. The people I spend two days with at institute programs are like family by the time we finish.

"For Today We'll Find A Way" *to get a little help from our friends for smoother sailing.*

December 25

"To the important Plus Factor add enthusiasm, intellectual competency, as well as spiritual thinking and you've got an unbeatable combination. You have the making of somebody special."
                                        -Norman Vincent Peale

Don't we all want to feel *special*? We are all part of a wonderful tapestry with many lives intertwined. Isn't it great that we can have such positive influences on the lives we touch?

When I was a young child, everyone explained my crazy ways by saying I was a free spirit. I like that explanation. To have spirit is what life's all about.

When we affirm each morning, what kind of day we want to have, it really makes our day somewhat predictable.

"For Today We'll Find A Way" *to see we are all very special and an important part of this universe. Happy holidays to you and yours.*

December 26

"When you talk about changing man (woman), you know it will require some force of enormous power to do so."   -Norman Vincent Peale

Recently, on an ACOA retreat, Father Lutz told us this story. There were two twin brothers, one was always optimistic and one was always pessimistic. They decided to do a study to see if they could change them.

They bought the pessimist everything he ever wanted. The house was full of wonderful gifts. He opened each gift with comments like, "I don't like the color, or I had another style in mind."

They then told the other twin that his present was out in the shed. They went out to see his reaction. He was all excited and happy. Manure was flying all over the shed and they asked, "Do you like you present?" He replied, "Oh, it's okay, but with all the manure, there's bound to be a pony in here somewhere."

"For Today We'll Find A Way" *for our minds are a powerful force. We can be optimistic, if we work at it.*

December 27

"Today the real achievers are excited, enthusiastic participants and leaders in creativity."
                    -Norman Vincent Peale

I have had the opportunity of taking a color class from Penny Parker. She makes color easy to understand, and brings out the creative touch we all have as hairdressers.

Another person that has brought out my creativity is Paula Henry. Here's a lady who can teach us how to project what we want to say in an exciting way so people will want to listen.

Whether we are learning color or public speaking, let's find a way to see the wonderful creativity in our industry. There are so many people willing to help us if we seek them out.

Enthusiasm for education in our industry, is what makes opening my salon each day fun.

"For Today We'll Find A Way" *to be CREATIVE!*

December 28

"Emotion follows thought."   *-Jacquelyn Small*

    Here is a poem written by a nice young man with good values and a kind heart. He wrote it for Stacey Evenson, one of our team members.

Different than ever before or any other time
I've got this lovely lady on my mind.
Fantastic feelings and an excellent notion
encompassed by romantic emotions.
Not sure what's happening to me
thoughts connected to her with everything I see.
I ask myself, what could this be?
My only conclusion is that this is intense
this coming from a person normally on defense.
Oh my, good love songs are making sense.
                                            -Jim Arvigo

"For Today We'll Find A Way" *for our emotion to flow with love for each other.*

December 29

"The ultimate weapon is a well trained soldier."
-General George S. Patton

As we approach the New Year are we ready for positive change? Dreams, goals and a plan in place?

Dennis Millard is a man who cares about the next guy and I feel fortunate that he taught me how to achieve my goals.

We are all lucky if we each find a few friends in a lifetime. The people I have shared with you in this book are genuine and have big hearts. To be a well trained soldier is the only answer. We can't achieve our goals just by wishing and hoping. If we make the effort to educate ourselves, our salon industry will be stronger and better. Success is simple when we take the effort to continue to train ourselves.

"For Today We'll Find A Way" *to dream, set our goals and have our plan. We're in this together!*

December 30

"Our simple objective is finding a way to win - for fun and profit."   *-Dan O'Brien*

As we embark on our mission of shaping our future together, the most important factor is to enjoy what we're doing.

Most of my life I worked very hard to survive. I'm learning to work smart not hard.

I knew the first time I saw my mom's hair done professionally, that was what I wanted to do. We must be very sure. The tools of success are many, and remember, a long journey starts with a single step.

In sharing my thoughts with you, remember, if there's a problem, there's *always* a solution.

You can't possibly get anything without giving it back.

"For Today We'll Find A Way" to win and have fun and profit on the way.

December 31

"Winners never quit and quitters never win."
-Florence Chadwick

Times are always changing, and by networking with wonderful friends I've made, I am always getting new ideas. Ask winners for ideas.

Emmy and Heidi have always been a great source of support for me. They work together in a salon named Exclusiva near Milwaukee. They gave me great promotional ideas.

Since our slow times are in January and February, they suggested giving clients a $5 discount for each of those months. It really generates more business for us and I thank them.

These are the high caliber people you meet while attending programs by Dr. Lew, Carole and Dennis. It all starts with commitment. If we are committed to our own success, we will have it.

"For Today We'll Find A Way" *to start a new beginning. It's time for a fresh outlook! Happy New Year!*